Jacqueline Novels
12/30/10

ONE YEAR
WITH JESUS

365 DEVOTIONAL THOUGHTS ON THE RED LETTER WORDS

D0633057

JAMES A. DAVEY

BARBOUR
PUBLISHING

© 2011 by James A. Davey

ISBN 978-1-60260-893-1

Published by Barbour Publishing, Inc., P.O. Box 719, Uhrichsville, Ohio 44683 www.barbourbooks.com

Our mission is to publish and distribute inspirational products offering exceptional value and biblical encouragement to the masses.

ecpa Member of the
Evangelical Christian
Publishers Association

Printed in the United States of America.

INTRODUCTION

Overflowing with insight, yet divided into readings that are clear and concise, this 365-day devotional will take you to the side of Jesus, where the best learning occurs. What could be better than spending one year with Jesus—learning from His own words what He wants for your life? Hear His advice to His followers, listen in on His conversations with the disciples, eavesdrop as He teaches the children, and marvel as He speaks on the cross. Truly, nothing is so profound as the words of the Savior!

*"Why were you searching for me?"
he asked. "Didn't you know I had
to be in my Father's house?"*
LUKE 2:49

In His first recorded words, the twelve-
year-old Jesus demonstrated a remarkable
clarity about who He was, His mission, and
His purpose. As you begin this year-long
journey, ask God to do the same for you.

Mission/ Purpose
For Jesus to be
increase and I
decrease. The glory
of God be revealed in me.
John 3:30

DAY
2

*But Jesus told him, "No! The Scriptures
say, 'People do not live by bread alone,
but by every word that comes from
the mouth of God.'"*
MATTHEW 4:4 NLT

The Bible is a book like other books, but
it is not *just* like other books. It is much
more. It will nourish and sustain your inner
spiritual life and make you strong when and
where it counts the most. Read the Bible
today and every day.

DAY
3

It is written, Thou shalt worship the Lord thy God, and him only shalt thou serve.
LUKE 4:8 KJV

We worship that to which we attribute ultimate worth. This is a sobering word to all of us who live in a culture enamored with physical beauty, pleasure, power, and wealth. These are all temporary; don't give them an importance that is godlike.

**DAY
4**

*Jesus answered, "It says: 'Do not put the
Lord your God to the test.'"*
LUKE 4:12

God will not be trifled with. He will bear with
your honest questions, your doubts, and
even your blind anger. But He will not be
used, and He cannot be tricked into being
an agent of your selfish desires.

Jesus looked around and saw them following. "What do you want?" he asked them. They replied, "Rabbi" (which means "Teacher"), "where are you staying?" "Come and see," he said.
JOHN 1:38–39 NLT

Following Jesus is a journey of discovery. We don't know at the outset all that we may find or when the discoveries will be made. Just keep Jesus in sight, and go today where He will lead.

*The day following Jesus would go forth into
Galilee, and findeth Philip, and saith unto
him, Follow me.*
JOHN 1:43 KJV

We sometimes think that spiritual living
must be complex and difficult. There
must be so many rules to be obeyed
and so many rituals that require timely
performance. We fear boredom and all
external constraints. I have good news!
The rule for spiritual living is simple and
singular: Follow Jesus!

Jesus said to the servants, "Fill the jars with water"; so they filled them to the brim. Then he told them, "Now draw some out and take it to the master of the banquet." They did so, and the master of the banquet tasted the water that had been turned into wine.
JOHN 2:7–9

Filling a jar with water doesn't sound very spiritual. But often it is in the most common daily tasks that we find ourselves surprised and delighted to discover that God has worked a miracle. In whatever you have to do today, expect God to show up!

DAY
8

Jesus replied, "I tell you the truth, unless you are born again, you cannot see the Kingdom of God."
JOHN 3:3 NLT

Transformation is the goal of this one-year journey with Jesus. It's a new beginning, a fresh start, a clean sheet of paper. Today, give Him the old, worn, muddied pages of your past. He knows what to do with your sins and failures. Be born anew today.

And as Moses lifted up the serpent in the wilderness, even so must the Son of man be lifted up: that whosoever believeth in him should not perish, but have eternal life.
JOHN 3:14–15 KJV

The cross was no accident. In the long reaches of time, it was a good day, hence *Good Friday*. The cross marked a sacrifice by a Savior. Jesus *must* be lifted up, that believing, you may have eternal life.

DAY 10

"For God so loved the world that he gave his one and only Son, that whoever believes in him shall not perish but have eternal life."
JOHN 3:16

Pick out the most important word in this best-loved verse of scripture and think about it today: God *loved* the world! And He loves you.

"All who do evil hate the light and refuse to go near it for fear their sins will be exposed. But those who do what is right come to the light so others can see that they are doing what God wants."
JOHN 3:20–21 NLT

Here's a simple observation of human nature. We hide those thoughts and actions that reflect badly on us. But where shame and guilt are absent, we are free to live with transparency. Only as we allow God to work in us (and on us) can we come out of the shadows and live in the open.

DAY
12

Jesus answered and said unto her, If thou knewest the gift of God, and who it is that saith to thee, Give me to drink; thou wouldest have asked of him, and he would have given thee living water.
JOHN 4:10 KJV

You, too, are surrounded at this moment by infinite possibilities, which Jesus described as "the gift of God." Look for God in the everyday, mundane experiences of life. Be on the lookout today!

"Whoever drinks the water I give him will never thirst. Indeed, the water I give him will become in him a spring of water welling up to eternal life."
JOHN 4:14

There is spiritual thirst in every person. It can be temporarily quenched by noble pursuits as well as by frantic activity and mindless entertainment. It reappears, however, at inconvenient and sometimes unsettling moments. Jesus offers more than a temporarily satisfying drink; He is a living spring!

DAY 14

"But the time is coming—indeed it's here now—when true worshipers will worship the Father in spirit and in truth. The Father is looking for those who will worship him that way."
JOHN 4:23 NLT

Here's an interesting thought to ponder: The heavenly Father is seeking you today as much, or more, than you are seeking Him! Surely you will find Him as you open your whole person to Him and invite Jesus in.

God is a Spirit: and they that worship him must worship him in spirit and in truth.
JOHN 4:24 KJV

The Spirit of God draws us to truth. The more truth we live, the more we are drawn to the Spirit. Real worship is not mechanical or rote, nor is it habit or tradition. It is our inner response to the deepest callings of God on our lives.

DAY
16

*"Open your eyes and look at the fields!
They are ripe for harvest."*
JOHN 4:35

We may think that other people have their
lives together and only we have nagging
inner hungers. The reality is that people
everywhere need Christ. Someone whose
path you will cross today may be ready
to hear what you are experiencing about
Jesus, so be prepared.

DAY
17

"The time promised by God has come at last!"
he announced. "The Kingdom of God is near!
Repent of your sins and believe the Good News!"
MARK 1:15 NLT

To repent is to reverse course, to turn
around, to turn away from what is known to
be wrong and to embrace what is known
to be right. Is it time for you to repent?

DAY
18

And he said, Verily I say unto you,
No prophet is accepted in his own country.
LUKE 4:24 KJV

The hardest place to let your light shine is
at home. This is where people know you
best, know your background, and know
your faults. But no place is more important
than with those you love. If the light doesn't
shine at home, there is little use taking it to
a faraway place.

*"Come, follow me," Jesus said,
"and I will make you fishers of men."*
MARK 1:17

True followers of Jesus attract others to
Him. Problems arise when we set out to
attract others while not following Jesus or
while following at a distance. Concentrate
on following Jesus as closely as possible,
and you will be amazed at how He will
make you a good fisherman.

But Jesus replied, "We must go on to other towns as well, and I will preach to them, too. That is why I came."
MARK 1:38 NLT

Jesus was never satisfied to settle down in one place, enjoying success and perhaps building a monument to His own accomplishment. There was always the restless call of the "others." So it is with you. The life of following Jesus is not only to be enjoyed; it is to be shared.

And it came to pass, when he was in a certain city, behold a man full of leprosy: who seeing Jesus fell on his face, and besought him, saying, Lord, if thou wilt, thou canst make me clean. And he put forth his hand, and touched him, saying, I will: be thou clean. And immediately the leprosy departed from him.
LUKE 5:12–13 KJV

When we draw near to Jesus, we need never wonder if He cares about our troubles or if He is willing to help us. His willingness should never be the issue, though our reluctance to come to Him often is!

DAY
22

*Some men brought to him a paralytic, lying
on a mat. When Jesus saw their faith, he
said to the paralytic, "Take heart, son;
your sins are forgiven."*
MATTHEW 9:2

The most apparent need is not always the
most important or core issue. There's a
good chance that the matter concerning
you most today is not the one Jesus knows
to be your greatest need. Trust Him to get
to the heart of the matter.

"Is it easier to say to the paralyzed man 'Your sins are forgiven,' or 'Stand up, pick up your mat, and walk'? So I will prove to you that the Son of Man has the authority on earth to forgive sins." Then Jesus turned to the paralyzed man and said, "Stand up, pick up your mat, and go home!"
MARK 2:9–11 NLT

Forgiveness was the issue; healing was a distraction. Jesus eventually forgave and healed. Many times the deep, inner work of forgiveness must be realized before there can be any substantial change in our more visible concerns.

DAY
24

*And as Jesus passed forth from thence, he
saw a man, named Matthew, sitting at the
receipt of custom: and he saith unto him,
Follow me. And he arose, and followed him.*
MATTHEW 9:9 KJV

Something about Jesus communicated
two things to Matthew. First, Jesus had
authority to issue a life-changing call,
and second, following Jesus would be
worth more to Matthew than any business
transactions he could complete that day.
Are you learning the same?

*Jesus said, "It is not the healthy
who need a doctor, but the sick."*
MATTHEW 9:12

The hardest accomplishment for a sick
person, often, is to admit the need for a
doctor! Maybe the illness will get better
by itself. But only a confession of need
brings us to the doctor. It's the same in
our spiritual lives. Getting to the point of
admitting a deep spiritual need is often
very hard. Tell Jesus today how much
you really need Him.

*Then Jesus gave them this illustration:
"No one tears a piece of cloth from a
new garment and uses it to patch an old
garment. For then the new garment would
be ruined, and the new patch wouldn't
even match the old garment."*
LUKE 5:36 NLT

What our souls need is not a little patch
here and there or a bit of renovation or
new resolution. Let's face it: We need to
be made new. And that is Jesus' specialty!
Don't seek incremental improvement; ask
for a total and extreme makeover!

*When Jesus saw him lie, and knew that he had
been now a long time in that case, he saith
unto him, Wilt thou be made whole?*
JOHN 5:6 KJV

As long as we are content to be as we
are, or to be less than God can make us,
we will never change. So the question
to ponder is the one Jesus asked. "Do
you want to be forgiven; do you want to
change; do you want to be done
with past failures and sins?"

DAY
28

"I tell you the truth, the Son can do nothing by himself; he can do only what he sees his Father doing, because whatever the Father does the Son also does."
JOHN 5:19

Apparently God has a kind of "family style." Jesus, the Son of God, lived in dependence upon His Father, doing what He would do. The clear implication is that we are to share this "style," living today and every day in conscious dependence upon Jesus.

*"For the Father loves the Son and shows
him everything he is doing. In fact, the Father
will show him how to do even greater works
than healing this man. Then you will truly be
astonished. For just as the Father gives life
to those he raises from the dead, so the Son
gives life to anyone he wants."*

JOHN 5:20–21 NLT

We are intrigued by the mystery and power
of a miracle. We should be truly amazed,
however, at the transformation of lives
to which Jesus gives life! The power of a
changed life is greater than any miracle.
"Lord, change me today."

DAY
30

*"I tell you the truth, those who listen to
my message and believe in God who sent
me have eternal life. They will never be
condemned for their sins, but they have
already passed from death into life."*
JOHN 5:24 NLT

Eternal life is not just something to look
forward to—it is something we are given
when we believe in Jesus. Do you believe
in Him? Are you putting your whole trust
in Him? According to His word, you have
crossed over into real life. You can take
His word for it!

*"I seek not to please myself
but him who sent me."*
JOHN 5:30

Immature people live to please themselves;
just watch any baby. Maturity is the ability
to defer our desires; just watch any mother!
Divinity gets beyond self to help others;
just watch Jesus.

DAY 32

Feb 11

"You search the Scriptures because you think they give you eternal life. But the Scriptures point to me! Yet you refuse to come to me to receive this life."
JOHN 5:39–40 NLT

The scriptures are an incredible treasure. Never underestimate the value of the Bible. But don't be content just to possess the Word, or even to understand it. In the Bible we meet the One who gives life. Knowing God through Jesus is the true prize.

DAY 33

And he said unto them, The sabbath was made for man, and not man for the sabbath: therefore the Son of man is Lord also of the sabbath.
MARK 2:27–28 KJV

Recapturing a "sabbath" as a day of rest and worship will not be done by instituting a maze of rules about what can and can't be done. Make Jesus Lord of every day of the week by keeping Him central to your thoughts and activities. Discover the joys of "sabbath."

Jesus knew what they were thinking and said to the man with the shriveled hand, "Get up and stand in front of everyone." So he got up and stood there. . . . [Jesus] said to the man, "Stretch out your hand." He did so, and his hand was completely restored.
LUKE 6:8, 10

Chances are, it wasn't easy for this man to stand and stretch out the very limb he had been seeking to hide. Neither is it easy for us to uncover our faults and limitations and reach out to Jesus. It is, however, the road to recovery and restoration.

DAY
35

*"God blesses those who are poor
and realize their need for him,
for the Kingdom of Heaven is theirs."*
MATTHEW 5:3 NLT

True happiness depends far more on
character than cash. Poverty of spirit is not
a bad self-image. It is a realistic appraisal of
self that causes people to seek God.
It is the condition of heart that God honors
and to which He responds. Be lifted up
by bending low before Him.

Blessed are they that mourn:
for they shall be comforted.
MATTHEW 5:4 KJV

The longer we live, the more evidence we collect that loss and diminishment lead to mourning. It is also true that when we mourn, we are comforted by those who care and gather around us. Who needs your comfort today?

*"Blessed are the meek,
for they will inherit the earth."*
MATTHEW 5:5

Meekness is power under control;
it is strength directed to a good end;
it is energy that is focused. It is no wonder,
then, that the meek will inherit the earth.
Meekness is the humility that permits the
Master to give it direction.

DAY
38

*"God blesses those who hunger and thirst
for justice, for they will be satisfied."*
MATTHEW 5:6 NLT

Hunger and thirst for righteousness are
urgent, intense longings to be like Jesus,
to be made new in His pattern. Only He
can live out the ideals of the Sermon on the
Mount, and only Jesus can make you what
you want to become.

DAY 39

Blessed are the merciful:
for they shall obtain mercy.
MATTHEW 5:7 KJV

Mercy stands in another person's shoes,
to understand and feel what he or she
does. Mercy deliberately identifies as
completely as possible and then responds
to benefit another at great cost to itself.
It is what God extended to us in Jesus.
Mercy given to others is good evidence
of mercy received.

Lamentation 3:22-23

DAY 40

*"Blessed are the pure in heart,
for they will see God."*
MATTHEW 5:8

God always goes for the heart. He is never
content to just dust us off, clean us up, and
tie us down to the externals of religious
practice. He seeks to get to the center of
our personality, the seat of our emotions,
and the source of our will. Only then will we
see God, and others see God in us.

DAY
41

*"God blesses those who work for peace,
for they will be called the children of God."*
MATTHEW 5:9 NLT

It takes people to make trouble, and it
will take people to make peace. You can
decide which you will do. Today as you
meet those who may be hostile, brittle,
or just different, seek to be at peace and
promote peace. It is the will of God,
and surely He will help you.

DAY 42

2/11

Blessed are they which are persecuted for righteousness' sake: for theirs is the kingdom of heaven.
MATTHEW 5:10 KJV

If you are feeling put upon or persecuted, check to make sure it's for the sake of righteousness and not for being overbearing, judgmental, or bad mannered! Your transparent walk with God acts as a silent rebuke to those who do not share your relationship with Jesus.

"Blessed are you when people insult you, persecute you and falsely say all kinds of evil against you because of me."
MATTHEW 5:11

Did you catch that key word? It's "falsely." If people have reason to say all kinds of evil against you, then the proper response is to apologize and make amends as quickly as possible. If you are in the crosshairs because of Jesus, you have the consolation that He is there with you.

DAY 44

2/13

Rejoice, and be exceeding glad: for great is your reward in heaven: for so persecuted they the prophets which were before you.
MATTHEW 5:12 KJV

The persecuted believer stands in the best of company. All the prophets, and even Jesus, were there before you. If that isn't enough encouragement to make you glad, contemplate your sure reward in heaven!

2/14

Ye are the salt of the earth: but if the salt have lost his savour, wherewith shall it be salted? it is thenceforth good for nothing, but to be cast out, and to be trodden under foot of men.
MATTHEW 5:13 KJV

How salty are you? You can help preserve all that is good around you. You can enhance the flavor of this day for your family, friends, coworkers, and neighbors. Don't lose your saltiness.

DAY 46

2/15

"You are the light of the world.
A city on a hill cannot be hidden."
MATTHEW 5:14

Everywhere you go today you carry spiritual
light. You may not even be aware of it.
The light seems brightest when we are not
consciously trying to be light. Light can
be hooded, it can be dimmed, it can be
shuttered and shaded, but it cannot be
extinguished.

2/16

DAY
47

"In the same way, let your good deeds shine out for all to see, so that everyone will praise your heavenly Father."
MATTHEW 5:16 NLT

You do not originate the light; you reflect it. This light is the illumination of God in you and through you. As you let the light shine all around you, remember that the praise belongs to your Father in heaven.

DAY
48

2/17

Think not that I am come to destroy the law, or the prophets: I am not come to destroy, but to fulfil.
MATTHEW 5:17 KJV

Imagine how miserable life would be if godlessness, murder, marital unfaithfulness, thievery, lying, and greed were not only sanctioned but celebrated by society! We seem to be living perilously close to such a world and need Jesus' reminder that God's standards have not been abolished.

2/18

*"I tell you the truth, until heaven and earth
disappear, not the smallest letter, not the least
stroke of a pen, will by any means disappear
from the Law until everything is accomplished."*
MATTHEW 5:18

God's moral standards never need to be
updated or modified. He still requires us
to be truthful, loyal in our commitments,
and honest in our dealings. The Ten
Commandments don't need to be etched
on the courthouse steps nearly as much
as they need to be installed as
the moral compass for our lives.

DAY
50

2/19

"So if you ignore the least commandment and teach others to do the same, you will be called the least in the Kingdom of Heaven. But anyone who obeys God's laws and teaches them will be called great in the Kingdom of Heaven."
MATTHEW 5:19 NLT

It is a dangerous illusion to think that some commandments are less important than others. It's a delusion to think we can teach others that some no longer apply and not be injured ourselves.

2/2v

DAY 51

Ye have heard that it was said by them of old time, Thou shalt not kill; and whosoever shall kill shall be in danger of the judgment.
MATTHEW 5:21 KJV

There are no laws against anger. But Jesus knew that whether it is the slow, smoldering kind of anger or the sudden, explosive kind, it can lead to the death of relationships as well as the loss of life. The inner life is where the big issues are dealt with, as evidenced by the need to invite Christ into our lives.

DAY 52

2/24

*"If you are offering your gift at the altar
and there remember that your brother
has something against you, leave your gift
there in front of the altar. First go and be
reconciled to your brother; then come and
offer your gift."*
MATTHEW 5:23–24

Some things are more important than just
another religious observance. Nothing is
more important than our relationships, both
with other people and with God. Take care
that relations are right, and only then will you
be free to offer your gifts, gladly, to God.

"When you are on the way to court with your adversary, settle your differences quickly. Otherwise, your accuser may hand you over to the judge, who will hand you over to an officer, and you will be thrown into prison. And if that happens, you surely won't be free again until you have paid the last penny."
MATTHEW 5:25–26 NLT

Our justice system seems to have interminable delays, resulting in outcomes that are distanced from the initial offense. Not so with God! Jesus would advise immediate action. Get right with God today. Tomorrow just might be a day late.

DAY
54

2/23

Ye have heard that it was said by them of old time, Thou shalt not commit adultery: but I say unto you, That whosoever looketh on a woman to lust after her hath committed adultery with her already in his heart.
MATTHEW 5:27–28 KJV

Thought is parent to the act. This rich insight into human nature is never so clear as in the case of the lustful mind. Bring the tapestry of your thoughts before God, and ask Him to forgive, cleanse, and elevate the imagery in your heart.

2/24

"If your right hand causes you to sin, cut it off and throw it away. It is better for you to lose one part of your body than for your whole body to go into hell."
MATTHEW 5:30

Sometimes nothing less than a shock treatment will drive a point home and make it stick. We have largely lost any sense of the seriousness of sin and the extent of its consequences. Don't cut off the hand; cut out the sin!

DAY
56

2/25

"You have heard the law that says, 'A man can divorce his wife by merely giving her a written notice of divorce.' But I say that a man who divorces his wife, unless she has been unfaithful, causes her to commit adultery. And anyone who marries a divorced woman also commits adultery."
MATTHEW 5:31–32 NLT

Are you contemplating divorce or know someone who is? If so, you know the importance of correct paperwork, understanding the laws, and following the rules. Please, before serving papers, pause long enough to listen to Jesus: There is hope and there is help.

DAY
57

But let your communication be, Yea, yea;
Nay, nay: for whatsoever is more
than these cometh of evil.
Matthew 5:37 KJV

A wonderful freedom comes when you say
what you mean and mean what you say.
Live so transparently that no one will need to
guess at either. Your word will be your bond.

DAY
58

2/27

*"If someone forces you to go one mile,
go with him two miles."*
Matthew 5:41

It takes a sturdy faith in God to believe
that, in the worst of circumstances—being
forced to go where you don't want to go
and do what you don't want to do—you
can be at peace. It may well be that in that
second mile God has purposed something
that will both delight and deepen you.

*"Give to those who ask, and don't turn away
from those who want to borrow."*
MATTHEW 5:42 NLT

It's clear that God loves generosity and
those who live that way. Someone today
will need your love, the encouragement of
your praise, the help of your resources, the
affirmation of your thanks, and the warmth
of your friendship. Don't turn away!

Mad
1

But I say unto you, Love your enemies, bless them that curse you, do good to them that hate you, and pray for them which despitefully use you, and persecute you; that ye may be the children of your Father which is in heaven: for he maketh his sun to rise on the evil and on the good, and sendeth rain on the just and on the unjust.
MATTHEW 5:44–45 KJV

Nothing speaks so loudly about man's true character as the way he treats his enemies. To seek the good of those who do you ill and to pray for the ones who put you down is to display the love of God. This is what He wants you to do, and He will help you.

3/2

"He causes his sun to rise on the evil and the good, and sends rain on the righteous and the unrighteous."
MATTHEW 5:45

It may seem that God is either careless or callous in His failure to mete out illness, misfortune, and loss to evil people, and to withhold success, prosperity, and health from some who are righteous. But all accounting in this world is preliminary and partial, so don't waste time fretting over apparent injustices.

DAY
62

3|3

*"If you love only those who love you, why
should you get credit for that? Even sinners
love those who love them! And if you do
good only to those who do good to you,
why should you get credit? Even sinners do
that much!"*
LUKE 6:32–33 NLT

Jesus knocks the pins out from under every
vestige of self-interest and self-absorption.
His focus was consistently on the "others."
He sought out the poor, the disadvantaged,
the suffering, and the sinful. He never did
anything to curry favor with the powerful
and influential, but loved those most who
could do the least in return.

3/4

Take heed that ye do not your alms before men, to be seen of them: otherwise ye have no reward of your Father which is in heaven.
MATTHEW 6:1 KJV

What God thinks about you is far more important than the opinions people may have. The reason is clear. People can see only the outward acts, while God knows your motivations. Nowhere is this more important than in the performance of your religious duties.

3|5 5

*"So when you give to the needy, do
not announce it with trumpets, as the
hypocrites do in the synagogues and on
the streets, to be honored by men. I tell you
the truth, they have received their reward
in full. But when you give to the needy, do
not let your left hand know what your right
hand is doing, so that your giving may be in
secret. Then your Father, who sees what is
done in secret, will reward you."*
MATTHEW 6:2–4

If you give to charitable causes in order
to have the recognition and admiration of
other people, you must calculate carefully
for maximum effect. Jesus advises a kind
of giving that, by comparison, is reckless
and uncalculated. But the Father
always knows.

3 | 6

"But when you pray, go away by yourself, shut the door behind you, and pray to your Father in private. Then your Father, who sees everything, will reward you."
MATTHEW 6:6 NLT

Prayer is essentially both a privileged and private conversation. Think of it! You converse with your heavenly Father, the God of creation and the possessor of infinite power. Privacy is needed so that you can tell Him those secrets you voice to none other.

DAY 66

After this manner therefore pray ye:
Our Father which art in heaven,
Hallowed be thy name.
MATTHEW 6:9 KJV

Prayer begins with recognition of the
holiness of God. When gripped by that
awareness, you will not ask for anything
unworthy of His character or beneath His
nature. The holy nature of God keeps us
honest with ourselves and modest
in our petitions.

3| -8

*"Your kingdom come, your will be done
on earth as it is in heaven."*
MATTHEW 6:10

No one questions that God's will is done in
heaven. There His kingdom qualities prevail
entirely. But what is a daily issue for us is
the doing of His will on earth.
More particularly, how will you
seek to do God's will today?

"Give us today the food we need."
MATTHEW 6:11 NLT

Most of our true needs recur daily. For
example, we need food and drink, air to
breathe, and health to live. Because we are
so regularly and abundantly provided for,
we may forget God's daily care. Find time
today to thank God for things most often
taken for granted.

3| 10

DAY
69

And forgive us our debts,
as we forgive our debtors.
MATTHEW 6:12 KJV

There is a deliberate linkage here that
cannot be evaded. Only when you have
forgiven those who have sinned against
you can you fully realize the freedom of
God's forgiveness of your sins.

DAY
70

"And lead us not into temptation,
but deliver us from the evil one."
MATTHEW 6:13

Jesus took the presence and power of
an "evil one" far more seriously than most
moderns. From what other source could
the snares of temptation come? Ask God
to lead you away from temptation and to
keep you when you are in it.

3/12

*"If you forgive those who sin against you,
your heavenly Father will forgive you."*
MATTHEW 6:14 NLT

It is not easy to forgive. Forgiveness is more
than forgetting, ignoring, or pretending that
the effects of injury done to you do not
exist. Forgiveness is a deliberate absorption
of the wrong done you, understanding its
full extent, and choosing to let it go.

3/13

But if ye forgive not men their trespasses, neither will your Father forgive your trespasses.
MATTHEW 6:15 KJV

What sobering words! Forgiveness is a choice; it can only be extended voluntarily. It cannot be demanded, earned, or legislated. Choose, then, to release those who have wronged you from the bondage of your anger. You will discover broken shackles at your own feet.

3/14

"When you fast, do not look somber as the hypocrites do, for they disfigure their faces to show men they are fasting."
MATTHEW 6:16

Fasting for more than vain, personal reasons is largely forgotten. Fasting is a voluntary relinquishment of our right to some necessity in order to concentrate on God for a time or season. As you spend this year with Jesus, consider where and how fasting might fit into your obedience.

DAY 74

3/15

"But when you fast, comb your hair and wash your face. Then no one will notice that you are fasting, except your Father, who knows what you do in private. And your Father, who sees everything, will reward you."
MATTHEW 6:17–18 NLT

A true fast can no more be advertised than it can be demanded. It is between you and God, period! When you choose to fast in order to attend more closely to God in prayer, do it carefully and tell no one. The only One who matters already knows.

DAY
75

*Lay not up for yourselves treasures upon earth,
where moth and rust doth corrupt, and where
thieves break through and steal.*
MATTHEW 6:19 KJV

The periodic downturns in market-driven
economies may have a redeeming feature
by reminding us that everything we store
up on earth is subject to loss and looting
of one kind or another. Hold your
"things" very lightly.

DAY 76

3/17

"But store up for yourselves treasures in heaven, where moth and rust do not destroy, and where thieves do not break in and steal."
MATTHEW 6:20

Heaven is the one secure repository for treasure. What you do today that has heavenly value and eternal quality can never be stolen or tarnished. What you give for God and His work is the only thing you will never lose.

3/18

*"Wherever your treasure is, there the desires
of your heart will also be."*
MATTHEW 6:21 NLT

Do you have trouble keeping your mind
on God and His work in the world? Try
giving yourself and your resources. Give
generously, even lavishly. When God has
your treasure, you will be surprised at how
easy it is to set your heart on Him.

*No man can serve two masters: for either
he will hate the one, and love the other; or
else he will hold to the one, and despise the
other. Ye cannot serve God and mammon.*
MATTHEW 6:24 KJV

Are you thinking today of quitting this "one
year with Jesus" and going back to "doing
your own thing"? You're at a crossroad.
Which master will you serve? Only you
can choose.

"Therefore I tell you, do not worry about your life, what you will eat or drink; or about your body, what you will wear. Is not life more important than food, and the body more important than clothes?"
MATTHEW 6:25

These are the very things we *do* worry about! And, yes, Jesus does understand. But you were made for eternity, not time alone. You are meant for far more than a short lifetime of good food and fine clothes. You are in training for everlasting life!

"Look at the birds. They don't plant or harvest or store food in barns, for your heavenly Father feeds them. And aren't you far more valuable to him than they are?"
MATTHEW 6:26 NLT

What busy people we are, frantically earning and setting aside today what we think we may need tomorrow. We worry about whether we have stored enough or if the barns are truly secure. And all the while the heavenly Father feeds us daily what we need.

DAY
81

Which of you by taking thought can
add one cubit unto his stature?
MATTHEW 6:27 KJV

Think of all the issues that have caused
you to worry through the years. Most of
them never came to pass, and the few
that materialized have been successfully
navigated. What are you worried about
today? Trust God, and go
forward in obedience.

"See how the lilies of the field grow. They do not labor or spin. Yet I tell you that not even Solomon in all his splendor was dressed like one of these. If that is how God clothes the grass of the field, which is here today and tomorrow is thrown into the fire, will he not much more clothe you, O you of little faith?"
MATTHEW 6:28–30

Do you have a little faith? That's all it takes to trust God. Look around you and see how God has regulated his world. Even wildflowers appear on schedule. And He will care for you. Trust Him with what faith you have.

DAY
83

"*So don't worry about these things, saying, 'What will we eat? What will we drink? What will we wear?' These things dominate the thoughts of unbelievers, but your heavenly Father already knows all your needs.*"
MATTHEW 6:31–32 NLT

What a comfort it is to know that your heavenly Father knows exactly what you need today. You may not know or think that you need far more than you really do. God has your true needs in clear view, and that's all you need to know.

DAY
84

But seek ye first the kingdom of God, and his righteousness; and all these things shall be added unto you.
MATTHEW 6:33 KJV

Here's a striking thought. If you set out to secure your "stuff," what you get is just "stuff." Set out to allow God's righteousness to establish His kingdom in your life, and you get God—and all the "stuff" you need besides!

*"Therefore do not worry about tomorrow,
for tomorrow will worry about itself.
Each day has enough trouble of its own."*
MATTHEW 6:34

One thing can be guaranteed throughout
this "one year with Jesus." Each day will
have its challenges and troubles. Don't
borrow from the future those troubles that
haven't yet come, and don't hang on
to the ones that are over.

DAY
86

"Do not judge others, and you will not be judged. Do not condemn others, or it will all come back against you. Forgive others, and you will be forgiven."
LUKE 6:37 NLT

We resent it when others judge our behavior. They cannot possibly know either the cause or the motivation. In spite of this, we judge, and sometimes condemn, other people, political positions, nations, and even family members. Set out today to forgive and not condemn.

Give, and it shall be given unto you; good measure, pressed down, and shaken together, and running over, shall men give into your bosom. For with the same measure that ye mete withal it shall be measured to you again.
LUKE 6:38 KJV

The law of reciprocity is nowhere more evident than in our giving. It's remarkable how often Jesus spoke of giving. It is a pretty good barometer of our spiritual health. "God, pry my fingers off the things I own, and teach me the joy of giving. Amen."

DAY 88

"Can a blind man lead a blind man? Will they not both fall into a pit? A student is not above his teacher, but everyone who is fully trained will be like his teacher."
Luke 6:39–40

We become like those who train us. That's why we resemble our parents and teachers. Ask yourself if you want your children or your friends to be just like you. This is one of the most powerful motivations to our personal spiritual growth.

DAY
89

"And why worry about a speck in your friend's eye when you have a log in your own?"
LUKE 6:41 NLT

In our own eyes, our personal failures are easily understood and thus excused. At other times, it is too painful to deal with the wreckage in our own lives. Before drawing attention to the faults of others, determine to identify and deal with your own.

*Either how canst thou say to thy brother,
Brother, let me pull out the mote that is in
thine eye, when thou thyself beholdest not
the beam that is in thine own eye? Thou
hypocrite, cast out first the beam out of
thine own eye, and then shalt thou see
clearly to pull out the mote that is in thy
brother's eye.*
LUKE 6:42 KJV

Jesus does not overlook the sins of others,
nor does He downgrade our desire to help
them. But what He insists on is the priority
of first dealing with our own sins and
shortcomings.

"Do not give dogs what is sacred; do not throw your pearls to pigs. If you do, they may trample them under their feet, and then turn and tear you to pieces."
MATTHEW 7:6

Some people are so resistant to God that the first words of testimony have no traction at all and may result in broken relationships. If you face such a person, cease talking and trust the power of consistent living.

DAY 92

"Keep on asking, and you will receive what you ask for. Keep on seeking, and you will find. Keep on knocking, and the door will be opened to you."
MATTHEW 7:7 NLT

Passivity is not a Christian virtue. Whether it is spiritual pursuit, sports, or business, reward comes to those who actively ask, seek, and knock. Relentless, persistent pursuit finds an open door, even in prayer.

DAY
93

Therefore all things whatsoever ye would that men should do to you, do ye even so to them: for this is the law and the prophets.
MATTHEW 7:12 KJV

The law of the land compels us to do no harm to others. Jesus compels us to do good! The first is negative; the second is positive. This "golden rule" gets us out of ourselves and puts us on the lookout for the good of others. Give a little kindness, encouragement, and care. Isn't that what you would like?

"Enter through the narrow gate. For wide is the gate and broad is the road that leads to destruction, and many enter through it."
MATTHEW 7:13

It's easy to do wrong. No one needs to be taught to lie, cheat, or steal. All too often, our moral "default position" leads us in the wrong direction. Majority opinion, if it is wrong, is not made right by being in the majority.

DAY
95

*"But the gateway to life is very narrow and the
road is difficult, and only a few ever find it."*
MATTHEW 7:14 NLT

Only Jesus is the gate to eternal life. It's
better to be on a narrow road with the
right guide and the best destination than to
travel the smoothest highway that leads to
the wrong destination. Get with Jesus,
and go with Him!

DAY
96

Beware of false prophets, which come to you in sheep's clothing, but inwardly they are ravening wolves. Ye shall know them by their fruits. Do men gather grapes of thorns, or figs of thistles?
MATTHEW 7:15–16 KJV

The daily headlines scream to us that things and people are not what they seem to be. Appearances often deceive. But the outcome of a life cannot be fabricated. Live today to produce good fruit.

*"Every good tree bears good fruit,
but a bad tree bears bad fruit. A good tree
cannot bear bad fruit, and a bad tree
cannot bear good fruit."*
MATTHEW 7:17–18

Jesus consistently emphasizes both the
inner life and external behavior. Human
religion tends to one extreme or the other—
embracing one and neglecting its opposite.
Neither, by itself, meets God's rigorous
standard. Be true all the way through!

DAY
98

"So every tree that does not produce good fruit is chopped down and thrown into the fire. Yes, just as you can identify a tree by its fruit, so you can identify people by their actions."
MATTHEW 7:19–20 NLT

No one speaks more of judgment and hell than Jesus. Life has consequences that are only fully realized in eternity.

Not every one that saith unto me, Lord, Lord,
shall enter into the kingdom of heaven;
but he that doeth the will of my Father
which is in heaven.
MATTHEW 7:21 KJV

Don't mistake spiritual fervor for relationship
with God. Religious language by itself earns
no favor with God. Don't settle for anything
less than the real deal—faith in Christ that
results in a walk pleasing to God.

"The good man brings good things out of the good stored up in his heart, and the evil man brings evil things out of the evil stored up in his heart. For out of the overflow of his heart his mouth speaks."
Luke 6:45

What have you been storing up within? Do you need to edit the TV you watch or the books you read? Do you need to make better choices in entertainment or on the Internet so that your overflow will be of good and not evil?

DAY
101

"So why do you keep calling me 'Lord, Lord!'
when you don't do what I say?"
LUKE 6:46 NLT

What a searching question! Isn't it
incongruous to call Jesus our Master
without a wholehearted obedience to Him?
You may not know His whole will for your
life—few do—but if you will obey what you
do know, He will make the rest clear.

DAY
102

*Whosoever cometh to me, and heareth my
sayings, and doeth them, I will shew you to
whom he is like: He is like a man which built
an house, and digged deep, and laid the
foundation on a rock: and when the flood
arose, the stream beat vehemently upon
that house, and could not shake it: for it
was founded upon a rock.*
LUKE 6:47–48 KJV

The foundations of a life are seldom
visible, but in a flood they are invaluable.
Dig deeper today into God's Word, the
Bible, and into God's way of prayer. You
will be shoring up your life so it can remain
unshaken when the torrents come.

"But the one who hears my words and does not put them into practice is like a man who built a house on the ground without a foundation. The moment the torrent struck that house, it collapsed and its destruction was complete."
LUKE 6:49

Collapse, destruction, and loss are always tragic however and whenever they occur. Often such disasters are preceded by steady erosion over time and the lack of preventive care. You can get ready today for tomorrow's tests by reading and understanding your Bible.

DAY
104

When Jesus heard this, he was amazed.
Turning to the crowd that was following
him, he said, "I tell you, I haven't seen
faith like this in all Israel!"
LUKE 7:9 NLT

Would you be amazed to discover that
people from a Christian tradition other than
your own will be in heaven? Consider that
they may be equally amazed to think that
you will be there! Faith in Christ, wherever
it is found, and in whatever form,
is rewarded by God.

DAY
105

And Jesus said unto the centurion, Go thy way; and as thou hast believed, so be it done unto thee. And his servant was healed in the selfsame hour.
MATTHEW 8:13 KJV

Some people never pray; others never act. There comes a point when prayer must yield to action. Having made our prayerful request and believing God has heard, we get up from our knees to go forward in faith.

DAY
106

*When the Lord saw her, his heart went out
to her and he said, "Don't cry."*
LUKE 7:13

Our Lord Jesus knows what makes us
weep. His compassion and mercy make
Him ready to step into our lives with healing
for our damaged emotions. Sense His
understanding and compassion for you
this very day.

Then he told John's disciples, "Go back to John and tell him what you have seen and heard—the blind see, the lame walk, the lepers are cured, the deaf hear, the dead are raised to life, and the Good News is being preached to the poor."
LUKE 7:22 NLT

Any authentic work of God inevitably reaches to the poor and neglected. Be wary of any religious effort that falls short of that. The good news of salvation is for all, not just the fortunate and the well connected.

DAY
108

For I say unto you, Among those that
are born of women there is not a greater
prophet than John the Baptist: but he that
is least in the kingdom of God is
greater than he.
LUKE 7:28 KJV

Maybe you feel you are "least" in the
kingdom of God. Be encouraged by these
words of Jesus. You are empowered by
the Holy Spirit within you to do great
things today.

*"To what, then, can I compare the people of
this generation? What are they like? They are
like children sitting in the marketplace and
calling out to each other: 'We played the flute
for you, and you did not dance; we sang a
dirge, and you did not cry.'"*
LUKE 7:31–32

Childish games are left behind, but game
playing often continues through adulthood.
We play games with spouses, employers,
teachers, and friends. We even think we
can play games with God! Remember that
He always has the last turn.

*"The Son of Man, on the other hand, feasts
and drinks, and you say, 'He's a glutton and
a drunkard, and a friend of tax collectors
and other sinners!' But wisdom is shown to
be right by the lives of those who follow it."*
LUKE 7:34–35 NLT

What Jesus' critics thought was such
a scandal was, and is, marvelously true
of Him. He is still a friend of those who
are scorned and helplessly in the grip of
addictive behaviors. He is your friend, too.

Then began he to upbraid the cities wherein most of his mighty works were done, because they repented not: Woe unto thee, Chorazin! woe unto thee, Bethsaida! for if the mighty works, which were done in you, had been done in Tyre and Sidon, they would have repented long ago in sackcloth and ashes.
MATTHEW 11:20–21 KJV

The old proverb is true, "A man convinced against his will is of the same opinion still." All the miracles we think would help us believe will do no good until our hard hearts are broken and true repentance for sin takes the place of stubborn pride.

*At that time Jesus said, "I praise you,
Father, Lord of heaven and earth, because
you have hidden these things from the
wise and learned, and revealed them
to little children."*
MATTHEW 11:25

Spiritual realities do not violate the intellect;
we are never asked to believe what isn't
true. But these same spiritual realities often
bypass the intellect, being discerned best
by those who, like children, believe with
simplicity and trust.

*"My Father has entrusted everything to me.
No one truly knows the Son except the Father,
and no one truly knows the Father except the
Son and those to whom the Son
chooses to reveal him."*
MATTHEW 11:27 NLT

No one has God figured out unaided.
The way to know God is to come to Jesus
and follow Him with trust and obedience.
As you do so, you will learn the Father's
heart and discover His way. Jesus chooses
to make God known to His own.

DAY
114

*Come unto me, all ye that labour and are
heavy laden, and I will give you rest.*
MATTHEW 11:28 KJV

Two small words are key to understanding
this marvelous promise. The first word is
"all." There are no exceptions, no special
hard cases. The second word is "will."
There is no *maybe*. Are you feeling weary
and burdened just now? Come to Him!

*"Take my yoke upon you and learn from me, for
I am gentle and humble in heart, and you will
find rest for your souls. For my yoke is easy
and my burden is light."*
MATTHEW 11:29–30

At first we think that submitting to Christ
will place an intolerable burden on us,
constricting our freedom. Only later we find
it easy and light, setting us free to reach our
true potential and our highest good.

DAY
116

Then Jesus answered his thoughts.
"Simon," he said to the Pharisee,
"I have something to say to you."
"Go ahead, Teacher," Simon replied.
LUKE 7:40 NLT

I wonder what Simon thought as he waited
for Jesus to speak. What do you think
Jesus would say were He to single you out
and talk to you alone? I'm quite certain that
before anything else, He would tell you just
how much He loves you.

*Wherefore I say unto thee, Her sins, which are
many, are forgiven; for she loved much: but to
whom little is forgiven, the same loveth little.*
LUKE 7:47 KJV

The more clearly we understand the reality
and magnitude of our sins, the deeper
will be our heartfelt gratitude for God's
forgiveness. Be set free by hearing His
words, "Your sins are forgiven."

*Jesus said to the woman, "Your faith has
saved you; go in peace."*
LUKE 7:50

Indeed, "Go in peace." Go in peace with
God, knowing that He has fully forgiven you.
Go in peace with others, empowered to love
and forgive. Go in peace within yourself,
free of haunting guilt and the necessity for
excuse making. The freedom of forgiveness
brings peace in all dimensions.

DAY
119

*"Similarly, a family splintered
by feuding will fall apart."*
MARK 3:25 NLT

A successful walk with God calls for a
singleness of heart that owns no higher
loyalty, permits no rival affection, and offers
no contrary obedience. Determine to follow
Jesus with an undivided mind.

DAY
120

He that is not with me is against me;
and he that gathereth not with me
scattereth abroad.
MATTHEW 12:30 KJV

There is no middle ground with Jesus.
Either you believe and follow or you tarry
and scatter. Don't look for a neutral place
or try to postpone your response. He loves
you and gave Himself for you; now give
yourself to Him.

*"And so I tell you, every sin and blasphemy will
be forgiven men, but the blasphemy against
the Spirit will not be forgiven."*
MATTHEW 12:31

Too many people are so caught up
in worrying about whether they have
committed an unpardonable sin that they
miss the assurance that "every sin and
blasphemy will be forgiven." Live this day in
the first phrase, not the second.

DAY
122

"And I tell you this, you must give an account on judgment day for every idle word you speak."
MATTHEW 12:36 NLT

Our words are a better indicator of who we really are than even our actions. Actions tend to be calculated; words are often careless. In either case, remember there is a day of judgment, a time of final reckoning.

But Jesus replied, "Only an evil, adulterous
generation would demand a miraculous sign;
but the only sign I will give them is
the sign of the prophet Jonah."
MATTHEW 12:39 NLT

The demand for a miraculous sign is
evidence of self-centeredness that puts us
in control of God. The resurrection of Jesus
after three days is all the evidence we need
to know that He is who He said He is—
God's only Son, our Lord.

DAY
124

"The men of Nineveh will stand up at the judgment with this generation and condemn it; for they repented at the preaching of Jonah, and now one greater than Jonah is here."
MATTHEW 12:41

Generally speaking, the issue of repentance does not turn on the presentation of more compelling evidence, but on our willingness to respond to what evidence we do have.

*There was a crowd sitting around Jesus,
and someone said, "Your mother and your
brothers are outside asking for you."
Jesus replied, "Who is my mother? Who are
my brothers?" Then he looked at those around
him and said, "Look, these are my mother and
brothers. Anyone who does God's will is my
brother and sister and mother."*
MARK 3:32–35 NLT

The family of God, which we know as the
church, with all its imperfections, is a great
gift and consolation. In believing, we are
linked to a new circle of family members
with Jesus Himself with us, as well.

DAY 126

Who hath ears to hear, let him hear.
MATTHEW 13:9 KJV

The issue is not human hearing or the
acuity of our auditory equipment. Jesus
knew that some people will always choose
not to hear, not to believe, not to obey.
Jesus appeals to the will, knowing full well
that some people only have a "won't"!

*"For I tell you the truth, many prophets and
righteous men longed to see what you see
but did not see it, and to hear what you hear
but did not hear it."*
MATTHEW 13:17

How privileged we are! Our spiritual
hungers are satisfied in having God's
Word—the Bible—being able to read it
and respond in faith. Not all people on
earth yet have such privilege. Can you
do anything about that?

DAY
128

"But since they don't have deep roots, they don't last long. They fall away as soon as they have problems or are persecuted for believing God's word."
MARK 4:17 NLT

Trouble and persecution either drive us closer to Jesus to find His strength, or they cause us to doubt and fall, thus demonstrating we had no rootedness in the first place.

*And these are they which are sown among
thorns; such as hear the word, and the cares of
this world, and the deceitfulness of riches, and
the lusts of other things entering in, choke the
word, and it becometh unfruitful.*
MARK 4:18–19 KJV

Life is always full of worries. You can count
yours. Wealth can deceive us into thinking
we are secure and need nothing and
no one. Our desire for our own way will
combine with worry and wealth to choke
back our spiritual hunger so that our lives
remain barren and empty.

DAY
130

"Others, like seed sown on good soil, hear the word, accept it, and produce a crop—thirty, sixty or even a hundred times what was sown."
MARK 4:20

The issue is not the fruitfulness of our lives, but the quality of soil we present the sower. The size of the crop is up to Him. Whether or not we produce a crop is up to us.

"*No one lights a lamp and then covers it with a bowl or hides it under a bed. A lamp is placed on a stand, where its light can be seen by all who enter the house. For all that is secret will eventually be brought into the open, and everything that is concealed will be brought to light and made known to all.*"

LUKE 8:16–17 NLT

Don't hide your walk with God. Let this "one year with Jesus" be transparent to other people. Talk to God about other people. Talk to other people about God.

*Take heed therefore how ye hear: for
whosoever hath, to him shall be given;
and whosoever hath not, from him shall be
taken even that which he seemeth to have.*
LUKE 8:18 KJV

The judgment of Jesus at first seems
manifestly unfair, until we realize that
listening is a continuing process, not a one-
time event. If we keep listening to Jesus,
we keep learning. If we stop listening, we
start losing what we already had.

DAY 133

"The owner's servants came to him and said, 'Sir, didn't you sow good seed in your field? Where then did the weeds come from?' 'An enemy did this,' he replied."
MATTHEW 13:27–28

Much like the owner's servants, we don't always realize there is an enemy of our souls. He is not all-powerful, but he is wily, relentless, and wicked. He seeks to choke off every holy impulse and block all spiritual progress. Resist him!

*"'An enemy has done this!' the farmer
exclaimed. "'Should we pull out the
weeds?' they asked. "'No,' he replied,
'you'll uproot the wheat if you do.'"*
MATTHEW 13:28–29 NLT

In our well-intentioned efforts to do right,
we can do damage, thus undermining the
very thing we seek to protect. Better to
trust God to preserve His interests and His
own people. At the last, He will judge
with absolute justice.

*And he said, Whereunto shall we liken the
kingdom of God? or with what comparison
shall we compare it? It is like a grain of mustard
seed, which, when it is sown in the earth, is
less than all the seeds that be in the earth: but
when it is sown, it groweth up, and becometh
greater than all herbs, and shooteth out great
branches; so that the fowls of the air
may lodge under the shadow of it.*
MARK 4:30–32 KJV

We live in an age that highly values size and
substance, rapid growth, and overpowering
strength. When the gospel is first planted
in our hearts, it seems initially to be
insignificant and weak. But give it time!
Allow God's good news to grow
in your life into all it can be.

DAY
136

"The kingdom of heaven is like treasure hidden in a field. When a man found it, he hid it again, and then in his joy went and sold all he had and bought that field."
MATTHEW 13:44

How much is it worth to have the burden of guilt and the weight of sin lifted? What would you give to find true joy, to possess an inner peace, and to live with a clear conscience? If there is anything you are holding back from God, it is likely to be the cost of kingdom treasure.

*"Again, the Kingdom of Heaven is like a
merchant on the lookout for choice pearls."*
MATTHEW 13:45 NLT

A great many people are looking for the right
thing in all the wrong places. Jesus is the
true pearl of great value. He can be found in
the pages of your Bible. He is clearly seen in
the lives He has touched. The church, often
misunderstood and maligned, is where
He lives within His people.

*Again, the kingdom of heaven is like unto
a net, that was cast into the sea, and
gathered of every kind: which, when it was
full, they drew to shore, and sat down, and
gathered the good into vessels, but cast
the bad away. So shall it be at the end of
the world: the angels shall come forth, and
sever the wicked from among the just.*
MATTHEW 13:47–49 KJV

Too many church problems are caused
by people trying to determine what fish
are bad and destined to be thrown away.
Leave the net alone! Resist the impulse to
judge. Any separation necessary will be
infallibly done by God at the end of the age.

"This is how it will be at the end of the age. The angels will come and separate the wicked from the righteous and throw them into the fiery furnace, where there will be weeping and gnashing of teeth."
MATTHEW 13:49–50

Whether this is a literal, fiery furnace or a terrifying figure of speech, it is a destiny no one should wish for herself or for her friends. Fortunately, this is not yet the end of the age. There is time to put your faith in Jesus, walk with Him, and follow Him.

*When Jesus woke up, he rebuked the wind
and said to the waves, "Silence! Be still!"
Suddenly the wind stopped, and there
was a great calm.*
MARK 4:39 NLT

Complete calm! Isn't that what we would
like to experience in the midst of our
storms? It is possible to be still when
everyone around you is thrashing about.
You can have peace inside while being
battered. Allow Jesus to speak His "Quiet!"
into your life today.

*And he said unto them, Why are ye so fearful?
how is it that ye have no faith?*
MARK 4:40 KJV

Fear is all the evidence we need for
deficient faith. By now we should be
further along in our spiritual journey, more
advanced in our walk with Jesus.
Spend less time with your fear
and much more with your faith.

DAY
142

"Go home to your family and tell them how much the Lord has done for you, and how he has had mercy on you."
MARK 5:19

Family should be the first to know. Have you told them of your desire to have this "one year with Jesus"? Tell them what insights you are getting and the progress you are making. You may be surprised to learn that your family has already noted that you have been with Jesus.

*But Jesus said, "Someone deliberately touched
me, for I felt healing power go out from me."*
LUKE 8:46 NLT

This was not a mere physical touch; Jesus
was being jostled by a crowd. In the middle
of that busy, earnest, churning crowd, a
woman who was least likely to succeed
reached out in faith, and power flowed
into her life from Jesus.

DAY
144

And when the woman saw that she was not hid, she came trembling, and falling down before him, she declared unto him before all the people for what cause she had touched him, and how she was healed immediately. And he said unto her, Daughter, be of good comfort: thy faith hath made thee whole; go in peace.
LUKE 8:47–48 KJV

It is never easy to speak out in the presence of others. The possibility of misunderstanding is high, making true transparency a risky venture. However, if God is at work in your life, perhaps healing you in some way, it is important that you speak up. Don't let people mistake the work of God for a run of good luck!

DAY
145

*Ignoring what they said, Jesus told the
synagogue ruler, "Don't be afraid; just believe."*
MARK 5:36

In order to make spiritual progress, we
must sometimes ignore what others say
and do. Their opinions are just that—
opinions. Don't let others' lack of faith put
a chill on your own faith or dampen your
ardor for an authentic walk with God.
What other people think of you
can seldom harm you. Just keep believing.

DAY
146

But the crowd laughed at him because they all knew she had died. Then Jesus took her by the hand and said in a loud voice, "My child, get up!"
LUKE 8:53–54 NLT

When we underestimate the power of God, we run the risk of "knowing" things that aren't necessarily true. The laughter quickly turned to awe and wonder. Let God into the hardest corner of your life. You are likely to find He will take you, too, by the hand.

*And when he was come into the house,
the blind men came to him: and Jesus saith
unto them, Believe ye that I am able to do this?
They said unto him, Yea, Lord.
Then touched he their eyes, saying,
According to your faith be it unto you.*
MATTHEW 9:28–29 KJV

Is there anything in your life right now that
you think is too big for Jesus to handle? The
likelihood is that what you experience with
God will be bound by the size of your belief.

DAY
148

*"Only in his hometown, among his relatives
and in his own house is a prophet
without honor."*
MARK 6:4

With laserlike clarity, Jesus exposes an
all too familiar human characteristic. Is it
possible that we discount what Jesus says
because we have heard so much about
Him through our lifetime? Try to listen
as you've never heard before.

DAY 149

He said to his disciples, "The harvest is great, but the workers are few."
MATTHEW 9:37 NLT

We sometimes question both ends of this statement. Those around us often seem resistant, and few of us suffer from a lack of clergy! Could it be that motivated and mobilized laity would result in a harvest that proves the point?

Pray ye therefore the Lord of the harvest,
that he will send forth labourers
into his harvest.
MATTHEW 9:38 KJV

When there is a spiritual harvest to be
brought in, it seems a bit limp to major
on prayer rather than action. But prayer
is needed to focus our attention, free us
from lesser concerns, and bring our own
devotion and deeds into conformity
to God's will.

"Freely you have received, freely give."
MATTHEW 10:8

God will never ask you to give what you
don't have, or to give more than you can.
His demands on you will be in perfect
balance with His investment in you.
He has given freely so that you
can respond in the same way.

DAY
152

"Look, I am sending you out as sheep among wolves. So be as shrewd as snakes and harmless as doves."
MATTHEW 10:16 NLT

Jesus always cared for His followers and warned them of sure dangers and spiritual predators. It is never wrong to be careful and thoughtful, and it is always right to be innocent of wrongdoing.

DAY
153

But when they deliver you up, take no thought how or what ye shall speak: for it shall be given you in that same hour what ye shall speak. For it is not ye that speak, but the Spirit of your Father which speaketh in you.
MATTHEW 10:19–20 KJV

Hard times may come to you, but always be aware that you do not face them alone. God has given His Holy Spirit to be with you and to equip you. Do not worry!

DAY 154

"All men will hate you because of me, but he who stands firm to the end will be saved."
MATTHEW 10:22

The more completely a follower of Jesus identifies with Him, the more likely that believer is to suffer with Him. But at the end of that temporary discomfort is a full salvation. Don't exchange that for momentary ease.

*"Students are not greater than their teacher,
and slaves are not greater than their master.
Students are to be like their teacher, and slaves
are to be like their master. And since I, the
master of the household, have been called
the prince of demons, the members of my
household will be called by even worse names!"*
MATTHEW 10:24–25 NLT

We have turned life upside down when we
who follow Jesus insist on taking the lead,
or seek to tell Jesus what to do and when
and how. Our proper role is to listen,
learn, and follow.

*And fear not them which kill the body, but
are not able to kill the soul: but rather fear
him which is able to destroy both soul
and body in hell.*
MATTHEW 10:28 KJV

Much of our life energy is spent in
protecting and preserving our physical
bodies. We forget that we are made
for another, better world in which the
consequences of this life are to be
played out.

*"Are not two sparrows sold for a penny? Yet not
one of them will fall to the ground apart from the
will of your Father. And even the very hairs of
your head are all numbered. So don't be afraid;
you are worth more than many sparrows."*
MATTHEW 10:29–31

An unacknowledged dread that stalks us is
the fear of insignificance, of not mattering.
Something in us wants to be meaningful.
What a comfort to know that our heavenly
Father values us enough to account
for every detail of our lives!

DAY 158

"If you refuse to take up your cross and follow me, you are not worthy of being mine. If you cling to your life, you will lose it; but if you give up your life for me, you will find it."
MATTHEW 10:38–39 NLT

The cross cost Jesus His life! As we take the cross into our own lives, we put to death our unholy desires and follow Jesus in a life of sacrificial service.

And whosoever shall give to drink unto one of these little ones a cup of cold water only in the name of a disciple, verily I say unto you, he shall in no wise lose his reward.
MATTHEW 10:42 KJV

The simplest task, done in Jesus' name, has enormous consequences and eternal reward. Seek not large and important work to do; find what needs to be done close to home and do it!

"Come with me by yourselves to a quiet place and get some rest."
MARK 6:31

Two things that almost always will dull and deaden your spiritual growth are the clamor of noise and the restlessness of weariness. Jesus wants you to find a quiet oasis today for rest with Him.

Late in the afternoon the twelve disciples came to him and said, "Send the crowds away to the nearby villages and farms, so they can find food and lodging for the night. There is nothing to eat here in this remote place." But Jesus said, "You feed them." "But we have only five loaves of bread and two fish," they answered. "Or are you expecting us to go and buy enough food for this whole crowd?"
LUKE 9:12–13 NLT

Often when we beg Jesus to do what we think is well beyond our capability, He turns the assignment back and asks us to do it. Do you face a difficult, embarrassing, or impossible situation today? Tackle it in the strength of Jesus and do it!

For they all saw him, and were troubled.
And immediately he talked with them,
and saith unto them, Be of good cheer:
it is I; be not afraid.
MARK 6:50 KJV

Events and situations overwhelm us when
we think we are all alone. Ask Jesus to
come aboard, and take courage. With
Him along, any journey goes better. Facing
some headwind today? Go ahead, ask Him
to come along!

*When the disciples saw him walking on the
lake, they were terrified. "It's a ghost,"
they said, and cried out in fear.
But Jesus immediately said to them:
"Take courage! It is I. Don't be afraid."*
MATTHEW 14:26–27

A great many things can terrify us, not the
least of which is an awareness of what we
don't understand. But when we let Jesus
step into those moments, He makes His
presence real and puts our hearts at rest.

DAY 164

"But don't be so concerned about perishable things like food. Spend your energy seeking the eternal life that the Son of Man can give you. For God the Father has given me the seal of his approval."
JOHN 6:27 NLT

It's good to have a realistic perspective on life. Most of what we work for is of limited life span and will soon spoil. Only the pursuit of God promises eternal permanence and God's seal of approval.

*Then said they unto him, What shall we do,
that we might work the works of God?
Jesus answered and said unto them,
This is the work of God, that ye believe
on him whom he hath sent.*
JOHN 6:28–29 KJV

Religion is incurably tied to the performance
of good works. It's all about what we do
to gain God's approval or what we shun to
avoid His condemnation. Jesus shatters
that mind-set with His emphasis
on belief and not behavior.

DAY 166

"I am the bread of life. He who comes to me will never go hungry, and he who believes in me will never be thirsty."
JOHN 6:35

Here's a promise you can take with you today and test for its durability and accuracy. Start your day by coming to Him. Live the day in moment-by-moment belief in Him. You will discover that your spiritual hungers and thirsts are truly satisfied.

*"However, those the Father has given me will
come to me, and I will never reject them."*
JOHN 6:37 NLT

You can never be so bad that Jesus will
turn you away. Your case is not (now, and
never can be) hopeless. Don't allow guilt,
fear, embarrassment, or anything else to
keep you away from Jesus. Your desire to
move close to Him is evidence
that the Father is drawing you.

*And this is the will of him that sent me,
that every one which seeth the Son, and
believeth on him, may have everlasting life:
and I will raise him up at the last day.*
JOHN 6:40 KJV

Scoop this truth up from the page and give
it a warm welcome in your heart. It is God's
will that you have eternal life and be saved.
So look to Jesus, the Son of God, and
believe in Him. Put your full trust in Him
for eternal salvation.

"I tell you the truth, he who believes has everlasting life. I am the bread of life."
JOHN 6:47–48

Do you still wonder that the gift of everlasting life is received only by faith in Jesus? Surely He, of all people, would not lie to you! Taste and see the true satisfaction there is in following Jesus.

"The Spirit alone gives eternal life. Human effort accomplishes nothing. And the very words I have spoken to you are spirit and life. But some of you do not believe me." (For Jesus knew from the beginning which ones didn't believe, and he knew who would betray him.)
JOHN 6:63–64 NLT

We think that surely our good behavior must count for something! Salvation by faith in Jesus must be helped along by what we do. But no, Jesus says, "The flesh counts for nothing." So stop disbelieving, take His word for it, and put your whole faith and belief in Jesus—plus nothing!

There is nothing from without a man,
that entering into him can defile him:
but the things which come out of him,
those are they that defile the man.
MARK 7:15 KJV

Religion occupies itself with regulating what
food and drink may be enjoyed, and when,
and how. Don't fool yourself into thinking
that such rules will set you free. The real
issue is what lies within you. It is inner
space that requires constant monitoring.

DAY
172

*"From within, out of men's hearts, come evil
thoughts, sexual immorality, theft, murder,
adultery, greed, malice, deceit, lewdness,
envy, slander, arrogance and folly. All these
evils come from inside and make
a man 'unclean.'"*
MARK 7:21–23

When we realize what litters our interior
landscape, we realize our need of an
"extreme makeover" of divine proportions.
Even when these evils are never acted out,
they can lay hold of the imagination
and thought life.

He replied, "You know the saying, 'Red sky at night means fair weather tomorrow; red sky in the morning means foul weather all day.' You know how to interpret the weather signs in the sky, but you don't know how to interpret the signs of the times!"
MATTHEW 16:2–3 NLT

"Red sky at night, sailor's delight; red sky in the morning, sailors take warning." It's important to read the weather around us, but it is more important to heed the signs God gives us to know the importance of the times in which we live.

*A wicked and adulterous generation
seeketh after a sign; and there shall no sign
be given unto it, but the sign of the prophet
Jonas. And he left them, and departed.*
MATTHEW 16:4 KJV

All the miracles in the world would be of
little hope and comfort apart from the
overwhelming evidence for the resurrection
of Jesus from the dead. It is that
resurrection that galvanized the wavering
disciples, and it is that resurrection that will
answer your doubts and questions.

On the way he asked them,
"Who do people say I am?"
They replied, "Some say John the Baptist;
others say Elijah; and still others,
one of the prophets."
"But what about you?" he asked.
"Who do you say I am?"
Mark 8:27–29

It's not enough to know what others think
of Jesus, however high they place Him
in their estimation. The real question is,
what do you believe about Him? Who is
He? Make Him your Savior and Lord
and be prepared to answer the question
with authority.

*"Now I say to you that you are Peter
(which means 'rock'), and upon this rock
I will build my church, and all the powers
of hell will not conquer it."*
MATTHEW 16:18 NLT

If the church was a human institution, it
would have disappeared a long time ago.
There is enough incompetence and venality
to doom the church to history's ash heap.
But it is His construction, and it is worthy of
your participation and allegiance.

*And when he had called the people unto him
with his disciples also, he said unto them,
Whosoever will come after me, let him deny
himself, and take up his cross, and follow me.
For whosoever will save his life shall lose it; but
whosoever shall lose his life for my sake and
the gospel's, the same shall save it.*
MARK 8:34–35 KJV

In the long history of Christian belief, many
have sacrificed their lives so that you might
believe. They have lost what they could not
keep and have gained what they cannot
lose. The price they paid is high,
but their gain is priceless.

*"If anyone is ashamed of me and my words
in this adulterous and sinful generation,
the Son of Man will be ashamed of him
when he comes in his Father's glory
with the holy angels."*
MARK 8:38

No one wants to be a spiritual exhibitionist.
But neither should we be ashamed to
acknowledge our allegiance to the Lord
Jesus Christ when the opportunity arises.
The stakes are too high.

*"The spirit often throws him into the fire
or into water, trying to kill him. Have
mercy on us and help us, if you can."
"What do you mean, 'If I can'?" Jesus asked.
"Anything is possible if a person believes."*
MARK 9:22–23 NLT

Most people live in the margin between
belief and unbelief. The corrective is
to admit the presence of persistent or
intermittent unbelief and pray for divine
help to turn that into a steady course of
believing. Let's be done with uncertain
and questioning faith.

DAY
180

And Jesus said unto them, Because of your unbelief: for verily I say unto you, If ye have faith as a grain of mustard seed, ye shall say unto this mountain, Remove hence to yonder place; and it shall remove; and nothing shall be impossible unto you.
MATTHEW 17:20 KJV

The effectiveness of faith is not due to how much we can muster up, but rather it relies entirely on the trustworthiness and power of the object of our faith. Don't put your faith in faith itself, but squarely on the mighty God who made and removes the mountains.

"From whom do the kings of the earth collect duty and taxes—from their own sons or from others?" "From others," Peter answered. "Then the sons are exempt," Jesus said to him. "But so that we may not offend them, go to the lake and throw out your line. Take the first fish you catch; open its mouth and you will find a four-drachma coin. Take it and give it to them for my tax and yours."
MATTHEW 17:25–27

In addition to the spiritual application, there is a powerful life lesson here. Nothing comes without effort or in the absence of focused work. Whatever coin you lack is best found by applying yourself to your work. Do that well, and you will be rewarded.

DAY
182

He sat down, called the twelve disciples over to him, and said, "Whoever wants to be first must take last place and be the servant of everyone else."
MARK 9:35 NLT

To be the servant of all is rarely why people want to be first. The values Jesus taught reverse the usual order. What is important is not our rank or standing, but what we do for others. And to be the servant of *all* is to not neglect the least, the last, or the lost.

And Jesus called a little child unto him, and set him in the midst of them, and said, Verily I say unto you, Except ye be converted, and become as little children, ye shall not enter into the kingdom of heaven. Whosoever therefore shall humble himself as this little child, the same is greatest in the kingdom of heaven.
MATTHEW 18:2–4 KJV

A child possesses an enormous reservoir of trust. We often call it gullibility or naïveté. Jesus knew that what is required to please God is not "street smarts" but an open, transparent belief of what we are taught in God's Word.

DAY
184

"If anyone causes one of these little ones who believe in me to sin, it would be better for him to have a large millstone hung around his neck and to be drowned in the depths of the sea."
MATTHEW 18:6

If you ever have reason to question the value of children, consider this warning. Children are far more than miniature grown-ups. It is a serious matter to harm or destroy the innocence of a child. We should aspire to share their childish, simple, uncomplicated faith.

"Anyone who is not against us is for us."
MARK 9:40 NLT

To listen to some religious arguments, it would seem that Jesus said, "Whoever is not for us is against us." Don't insist that everyone must see eye to eye on every doctrine, social issue, and personal practice. Live your spiritual life in a big tent!

*Moreover if thy brother shall trespass
against thee, go and tell him his fault
between thee and him alone: if he shall
hear thee, thou hast gained thy brother.*
MATTHEW 18:15 KJV

Don't harbor offenses. Don't keep a record
of transgressions and let it fester. Take
action sooner, rather than later, to seek
understanding and reconciliation. And
whatever you do, don't broadcast the
offense to all who will listen, thus
spreading the contagion.

"I tell you the truth, whatever you bind on earth will be bound in heaven, and whatever you loose on earth will be loosed in heaven."
MATTHEW 18:18

Earth is the arena in which we can and should act. Don't wait for heaven to do what needs to be done here and now. Act with care, knowing that what you do has eternal consequences.

DAY 188

"I also tell you this: If two of you agree here on earth concerning anything you ask, my Father in heaven will do it for you."
MATTHEW 18:19 NLT

Seeking the counsel and cooperation of another believer helps to moderate our more extreme wishes and refine and refocus our heart's desires. Find a faithful prayer partner, and you will be on the way to more fruitful living.

*For where two or three are gathered together in
my name, there am I in the midst of them.*
MATTHEW 18:20 KJV

We live in an age where bigness is valued for
its own sake. The risen Lord shows up just
as much in the smallest group of believers.
A company of only two or three won't make
much impression on the news, but it is Christ
in the midst who makes the difference.

*Then Peter came to Jesus and asked,
"Lord, how many times shall I forgive my
brother when he sins against me? Up to
seven times?" Jesus answered, "I tell you,
not seven times, but seventy-seven times."*
MATTHEW 18:21–22

The forgiving heart has no bottom to
its reservoir of mercy and cannot be
exhausted, any more than God puts limits
on His forgiveness. As long as we are
counting out offenses and marking the
number of our pardons, we are not
truly forgiving.

*Another said, "Yes, Lord, I will follow you, but
first let me say good-bye to my family."
But Jesus told him, "Anyone who puts
a hand to the plow and then looks back
is not fit for the Kingdom of God."*
LUKE 9:61–62 NLT

A decision to follow Jesus is almost always
followed by a multitude of distractions,
things to delay action or divert attention.
Determine today that you will follow Jesus,
and that nothing will cause you to look back.

DAY 192

Jesus answered them, and said, My doctrine is not mine, but his that sent me.
JOHN 7:16 KJV

It is very apparent that Jesus was always conscious of His dependence, day by day, on God the Father. His testimony was that even His teaching originated with the Father God. How very important then, that we take Jesus' words seriously and apply His teaching to our lives.

"If anyone chooses to do God's will, he will find out whether my teaching comes from God or whether I speak on my own. He who speaks on his own does so to gain honor for himself, but he who works for the honor of the one who sent him is a man of truth; there is nothing false about him."
JOHN 7:17–18

There is an internal consistency about an authentic Christian life. Nothing needs to be fabricated, or worse yet, hidden. The lack of pretense and the evidence of transparency is a winning combination. Don't fall for anything fake, false, or phony.

DAY
194

"Anyone who is thirsty may come to me!"
JOHN 7:37 NLT

It is one thing to have our thirst quenched.
It is something else entirely to be a thirst
quencher who brings relief to others all day
long. This reality is God's will for you today,
and if you will let Him, He will fill your life
with Himself to the point of overflow.

DAY
195

*So when they continued asking him,
he lifted up himself, and said unto them,
He that is without sin among you,
let him first cast a stone at her.*
JOHN 8:7 KJV

There is perverse satisfaction in condemning
someone else for her sin. How disappointing
then, to be reminded that our own sin
disqualifies us. Many stones of accusation
would drop from our fingers if we realized
that we deserve the same treatment.

*"Neither do I condemn you," Jesus
declared. "Go now and leave
your life of sin."*
JOHN 8:11

Forgiveness is free and clear, not
conditioned upon our behavioral change.
Precisely because we are forgiven and
know it, we are enabled to change. We
leave our sinful patterns behind us as an
expression of gratitude for God's
gift of grace.

*Jesus spoke to the people once more and said,
"I am the light of the world. If you follow me,
you won't have to walk in darkness, because
you will have the light that leads to life."*
JOHN 8:12 NLT

It is very frightening to be alone and in pitch
darkness—fear is resolved only when you
link up with someone who has a light on
the path ahead. Those who most closely
follow Jesus experience confidence,
clarity, and conviction.

DAY 198

*Then said Jesus to those Jews which
believed on him, If ye continue in my word,
then are ye my disciples indeed; and ye
shall know the truth, and the truth
shall make you free.*
JOHN 8:31–32 KJV

Curiosity for God's truth will take a person
only so far. A disciple does more than play
with Jesus' teaching. As you hold to the
teaching, you learn that the teaching holds
you and has the power to set you free
of guilt, shame, and fear.

*"So if the Son sets you free,
you will be free indeed."*
JOHN 8:36

No person is truly free who lives with dread
of the past or fear of the future. As we
allow Jesus to break the shackles of pride,
selfishness, sinful behavior, bad thoughts,
and impure motives, we feel ourselves
freed to serve others, love God, and be
what we were made to be.

"Which of you can truthfully accuse me of sin? And since I am telling you the truth, why don't you believe me?"
JOHN 8:46 NLT

It was true then, as it is today, that many people wanted to say nice things about Jesus and applaud His teaching, without ever taking that teaching and internalizing it. To refuse to believe it is to deny its truthfulness.

DAY
201

*Verily, verily, I say unto you, If a man keep my
saying, he shall never see death.*
JOHN 8:51 KJV

We dread death because it marks the
end of all we consider worthwhile. Jesus
assures us that death is rather a new
beginning. We will experience death, but
what we shall "see" is a fresh start.

*"Neither this man nor his parents sinned,"
said Jesus, "but this happened so that the
work of God might be displayed in his life."*
JOHN 9:3

Oh, that we might today display God at
work in our lives! How might He change us,
subtly reshape us, and refocus our aims?
Remove every blockade to His working
so that you may display His healing of will,
emotions, and body.

DAY
203

"We must quickly carry out the tasks assigned us by the one who sent us. The night is coming, and then no one can work."
JOHN 9:4 NLT

The onset of darkness comes on God's timetable, whether we have completed our chores or not. We may not know when it will turn to darkness, but we do know it is still light. Don't be one who spends the daylight trying to discover the timetable of darkness rather than using the light to prepare for it.

I am the door: by me if any man enter in, he shall be saved, and shall go in and out, and find pasture.
JOHN 10:9 KJV

This is the ironclad promise on which we stake our faith. Jesus alone is the gateway to eternal life. Don't ever waver on this point, and permit no substitutions, additives, or replacements.

DAY
205

*"The thief comes only to steal and kill and
destroy; I have come that they may
have life, and have it to the full."*
JOHN 10:10

Life with Jesus is no narrow, pinched,
desiccated experience. It is a full life. It is
to be a substantial model of what God
created life—and us—to be. All good things
are yours to be enjoyed.

DAY
206

"I am the good shepherd. The good shepherd sacrifices his life for the sheep."
JOHN 10:11 NLT

The shepherd understands he is there for the sheep; they are his mission. Their lives are in his hand. Their health and growth are his chief concern. Their enemies are his enemies, and he stops at nothing to see to his own sheep. In such manner, Jesus loved you and gave Himself for you.

*Therefore doth my Father love me, because
I lay down my life, that I might take it again.
No man taketh it from me, but I lay it down of
myself. I have power to lay it down, and I have
power to take it again. This commandment
have I received of my Father.*
JOHN 10:17–18 KJV

Don't think that the devil triumphed over
Jesus and trumped God's plan even
for one dark weekend! Jesus suffered
no defeat on the cross. The wonder of
salvation is that Jesus willingly chose the
humiliation and pain of the cross out of love
and obedience to the Father's plan.

*"Go! I am sending you out like lambs
among wolves. Do not take a purse or bag
or sandals; and do not greet anyone
on the road."*
LUKE 10:3–4

The stark contrast of our role as lambs
among wolves highlights the danger of
distraction. If we are concerned with
the issues of resources, supplies, and
equipment, we are not likely to survive
the well-meaning advice of our friends
along the way.

"I have other sheep, too, that are not in this sheepfold. I must bring them also. They will listen to my voice, and there will be one flock with one shepherd."
JOHN 10:16 NLT

Sermons and Bible studies are not to be trifled with! When truly centered on Jesus, they express His Word and will. If neglected, it is not the teacher who is turned away, or even Jesus the Son of God. A rejection of Bible truth is treated as a rejection of God Himself.

DAY 210

In that hour Jesus rejoiced in spirit, and said, I thank thee, O Father, Lord of heaven and earth, that thou hast hid these things from the wise and prudent, and hast revealed them unto babes: even so, Father; for so it seemed good in thy sight.
LUKE 10:21 KJV

Wisdom and learning are important but often overvalued. It is the openness of children, their tenderness of heart, and their transparency that can receive the truth of God.

*Then he turned to his disciples and said privately,
"Blessed are the eyes that see what you see.
For I tell you that many prophets and kings
wanted to see what you see but did not see it,
and to hear what you hear but did not hear it."*
LUKE 10:23–24

Jesus is the hope of the ages. The ancients
longed for a prophet to teach, a priest to
intercede with God, and a king to rule the
hearts of humankind. They waited in hope
and did not receive. It was to a small group
of humble disciples that God revealed
Himself in Jesus, and it is to humble
hearts that He still comes.

DAY
212

*But the Lord said to her, "My dear Martha,
you are worried and upset over all
these details!"*
LUKE 10:41 NLT

Some things are all right to do, but not
when better things are at hand. Why
fuss over the details of a dinner whose
nourishment is done in a day, when you
can listen to the Master whose words have
never faded? Try not to substitute good
things for the best things.

DAY
213

If ye then, being evil, know how to give good
gifts unto your children: how much more shall
your heavenly Father give the Holy Spirit
to them that ask him?
LUKE 11:13 KJV

The Holy Spirit is the best gift of all. He is
the gift that keeps on giving, the gift that
will not wear out, that cannot be outgrown
or done without. So ask! Ask for
the fullness of the Holy Spirit.

DAY
214

*"He who is not with me is against me, and
he who does not gather with me, scatters."*
LUKE 11:23

There appears to be no middle ground,
no disengaged neutrality. The last thing
anyone wishes is to be found in opposition
to the mighty God. Find out where God is
moving, and get with Him!

DAY
215

"No one lights a lamp and then hides it or puts it under a basket. Instead, a lamp is placed on a stand, where its light can be seen by all who enter the house."
LUKE 11:33 NLT

What we would never do in daily life we too often do in our spiritual lives. The light of Christ is to be displayed in our lives and on our lips. Displaying the light is our role. Dispersing the darkness is what the light will do.

DAY 216

But woe unto you, Pharisees! for ye tithe mint and rue and all manner of herbs, and pass over judgment and the love of God: these ought ye to have done, and not to leave the other undone.
LUKE 11:42 KJV

Don't be a Jesus follower who gets caught up in the minutiae of rules and rituals and has no time left to push for justice or show the love of God. Both are needed, and either without the other is insufficient.

"Woe to you Pharisees, because you love the most important seats in the synagogues and greetings in the marketplaces."
LUKE 11:43

There is something inherently out of whack when a follower of the humble Jesus seeks status and recognition. It is Jesus we hail. His honor and place in people's hearts are all that really matters.

DAY
218

"The time is coming when everything that is covered up will be revealed, and all that is secret will be made known to all. Whatever you have said in the dark will be heard in the light, and what you have whispered behind closed doors will be shouted from the housetops for all to hear!"
LUKE 12:2–3 NLT

That person is happiest who has nothing to hide and no reason to conceal. Live your life with as much transparency as you can muster, knowing that God notes every thought, hears every word, and observes every act.

*And I say unto you my friends, Be not afraid
of them that kill the body, and after that
have no more that they can do.*
LUKE 12:4 KJV

Most normal people fear pain, suffering,
and death. But there is something much
worse than the pangs of deprivation and
loss of life. We should live so that the worst
that could happen is that we die
and go to heaven for eternity.

DAY 220

"Indeed, the very hairs of your head are all numbered. Don't be afraid."
LUKE 12:7

Our God is the Lord of infinite detail and complexity. The God who knows the most minute detail of your life is He who designed the deep structure of all things. Knowing Him, through faith in His Son, Jesus Christ, is reason enough to shrug off our crippling fear and trust Him.

"And when you are brought to trial in the synagogues and before rulers and authorities, don't worry about how to defend yourself or what to say, for the Holy Spirit will teach you at that time what needs to be said."
LUKE 12:11–12 NLT

It is a great comfort to know that you have a Teacher residing within you who is adequate to help you in the worst of times. When you are at wit's end, you still have the inexhaustible resources of God to depend upon.

*And he said unto them, Take heed, and
beware of covetousness: for a man's life
consisteth not in the abundance of the
things which he possesseth.*
LUKE 12:15 KJV

There is the greed of the compulsive
acquirer who always requires more, and
there is the greed of the one who possesses
little but envies those with more. There is
also the greed of the one who, for pride's
sake, has chosen to live with less. Greed in
whatever guise is deadly to real life.

"But God said to him, 'You fool! This very night your life will be demanded from you. Then who will get what you have prepared for yourself?'
"This is how it will be with anyone who stores up things for himself but is not rich toward God."
LUKE 12:20–21

No matter how much of this world's treasured stuff you may collect, one thing is sure; you will leave it all behind some day. The only treasure that translates to eternity is what you send ahead by your investments in God's work in the world.

DAY
224

*Then, turning to his disciples, Jesus said,
"That is why I tell you not to worry about
everyday life—whether you have enough
food to eat or enough clothes to wear.
For life is more than food, and your body
more than clothing."*
LUKE 12:22–23 NLT

"Don't worry!" is one of the recurring
themes of Jesus' teaching. But how can
we stop? The ability to stop worrying lies in
gaining perspective on life itself. This is not
all there is! Food and clothing, no matter
how fine, will pass away, but life is forever.

*And which of you with taking thought can add
to his stature one cubit? If ye then be not able
to do that thing which is least, why
take ye thought for the rest?*
LUKE 12:25–26 KJV

The reality is that worry cannot add to your
life; it can only subtract. It will take away from
peace, it will stunt love, it will cripple faith.
Worry is destructive and corrosive. List your
worries, and then give them to God, asking
Him to exchange them for thankfulness.

DAY
226

*"You also must be ready, because the Son
of Man will come at an hour when you
do not expect him."*
LUKE 12:40

Be prepared today for the unexpected.
What is true in a general sense of the
return of Jesus to this earth is true in a
specific sense of every day. Be prepared
to be surprised by the good things that
will happen to you. The offering of human
kindness and the experience of God's love
may catch you unawares.

"But someone who does not know, and then does something wrong, will be punished only lightly. When someone has been given much, much will be required in return; and when someone has been entrusted with much, even more will be required."
LUKE 12:48 NLT

The plain fact is that we are stewards, not owners, of all that we are and have. Think about how you can use this very day—the resources and abilities entrusted to you—for God's glory and the good of others.

DAY 228

Or those eighteen, upon whom the tower in Siloam fell, and slew them, think ye that they were sinners above all men that dwelt in Jerusalem? I tell you, Nay: but, except ye repent, ye shall all likewise perish.
LUKE 13:4–5 KJV

Natural disasters, accidents, and sudden illnesses are not visited on people as a judgment from God. They do indicate the writhing of a world corrupted by sin and should lead us to repentance and faith while we still are able.

"Doesn't each of you on the Sabbath untie his ox or donkey from the stall and lead it out to give it water? Then should not this woman, a daughter of Abraham, whom Satan has kept bound for eighteen long years, be set free on the Sabbath day from what bound her?"
LUKE 13:15–16

Jesus showed little patience for man-made rules that keep people from doing what is truly important. Don't allow religious activity to multiply to the point that you have no time to help those who are most in need.

"My sheep listen to my voice; I know them, and they follow me. I give them eternal life, and they will never perish. No one can snatch them away from me."
JOHN 10:27–28 NLT

Jesus is more powerful than any enemy you can ever face. He is able to defeat the temptation that stalks you. He can break the habit that seeks to enslave you, and He will comfort you in your greatest loss and sorrow. You are absolutely safe in His hand!

*Strive to enter in at the strait gate: for many,
I say unto you, will seek to enter in, and shall
not be able. When once the master of
the house is risen up, and hath shut to the door,
and ye begin to stand without, and to knock
at the door, saying, Lord, Lord, open unto us;
and he shall answer and say unto you,
I know you not whence ye are.*
Luke 13:24–25 KJV

Here is another powerful reminder of the
importance of timely action. Don't delay!
While the door is open, while the way is
clear, while there is still time, let Jesus into
your life. He knocks now so that
you won't need to knock later.

"People will come from east and west and north and south, and will take their places at the feast in the kingdom of God. Indeed there are those who are last who will be first, and first who will be last."
LUKE 13:29–30

God's people are a multihued, multinationalistic, multiethnic multitude. Few of us have any idea how far the gospel has gone or how deeply it has penetrated. Be prepared for a delightful surprise at the heavenly feast to come.

"O Jerusalem, Jerusalem, the city that kills the prophets and stones God's messengers! How often I have wanted to gather your children together as a hen protects her chicks beneath her wings, but you wouldn't let me."
LUKE 13:34 NLT

Jesus offers us a protection good for time and eternity. It is an umbrella policy, good against all perils. But if you are not willing, if you reject His mercy and His grace, He will respect your right to choose. But why would you want to turn Him away?

DAY
234

For whosoever exalteth himself shall be
abased; and he that humbleth himself shall
be exalted.
LUKE 14:11 KJV

Better to humble ourselves than to be
humbled by others. Pride rarely recognizes
the limits of its own competence,
and so trips over itself.

"But when you give a banquet, invite the poor, the crippled, the lame, the blind, and you will be blessed. Although they cannot repay you, you will be repaid at the resurrection of the righteous."
LUKE 14:13–14

It's clear that God cares more than we do about the poor and those who are disadvantaged. Jesus also promises a blessing for joining Him in His compassion. Full payment awaits the resurrection, but down payments here and now are not unheard of.

DAY
236

*"And if you do not carry your own cross
and follow me, you cannot be my disciple."*
LUKE 14:27 NLT

Are you struck by the finality of the word
cannot that Jesus used? We like to think
that self-sacrifice is optional, that it is the
ultimate step in following Jesus. The truth
according to Jesus is that it is the first
and essential step.

For which of you, intending to build a tower, sitteth not down first, and counteth the cost, whether he have sufficient to finish it?
LUKE 14:28 KJV

If we should calculate the cost of earthly action, how much more should we carefully compute our willingness to carry our cross as we follow Jesus? For some, the cost may seem high and out of reach, but He always gives grace sufficient for every demand.

DAY
238

*"I tell you that in the same way there will be
more rejoicing in heaven over one sinner
who repents than over ninety-nine righteous
persons who do not need to repent."*
LUKE 15:7

God takes special delight in all His children,
but there is a heavenly party going on to
mark the salvation of men and women who
turn to God in repentance and faith. You
are invited to the party as you introduce
others to Jesus.

*"So he returned home to his father. And while
he was still a long way off, his father saw him
coming. Filled with love and compassion, he
ran to his son, embraced him, and kissed him."*
LUKE 15:20 NLT

Don't miss this: The Father is waiting; He
is watching; His heart is warm toward you;
and He is running to meet you much more
than halfway. He is prepared to
give you the greeting of your life!

DAY
240

And bring hither the fatted calf, and kill it;
and let us eat, and be merry: for this my
son was dead, and is alive again;
he was lost, and is found. And they
began to be merry.
LUKE 15:23–24 KJV

What a stark contrast between death and
life, between lostness and being at home!
That is the difference Jesus makes in
our lives. Invite Him in, and discover the
wonder of being made new. You will be
"at home" at last.

"Whoever can be trusted with very little can also be trusted with much, and whoever is dishonest with very little will also be dishonest with much."
LUKE 16:10

Deal with scrupulous care in the smallest of matters, the things no one else sees. Allow no compromise or collapse of conviction. When opportunity comes to deal with great matters, you will live in confidence and inspire the same in others.

"No one can serve two masters. For you will hate one and love the other; you will be devoted to one and despise the other. You cannot serve both God and money."
LUKE 16:13 NLT

If you are wavering in your desire to complete this "one year with Jesus," you understand the tension Jesus described. Perhaps it is time to recommit to the discipline of spending this daily time with Jesus. Leave no escape route or alternate plan.

DAY
243

And he said unto them, Ye are they which justify yourselves before men; but God knoweth your hearts: for that which is highly esteemed among men is abomination in the sight of God.
LUKE 16:15 KJV

It is an awesome thought that God knows the true motivations that drive us forward. We seek to package ourselves for the eyes of others and put the most favorable "spin" on our actions, but God is never fooled, and He cannot be "spun."

DAY
244

"So watch yourselves."
LUKE 17:3

Too many people spend their time watching
others, pointing out their flaws and
shortcomings. They are quick to condemn
in others the very traits they may display
themselves. Better to watch ourselves and
demand adherence to God's standards.
God will take care of everyone else.

"So watch yourselves! If another believer sins, rebuke that person; then if there is repentance, forgive. Even if that person wrongs you seven times a day and each time turns again and asks forgiveness, you must forgive."
LUKE 17:3–4 NLT

Don't make him repent seven times if he has only sinned against you once! Be as quick to forgive as you would like your foe to be quick to repent. The goal is restored fellowship, and that calls for a tender conscience and a merciful heart.

DAY 246

So likewise ye, when ye shall have done all those things which are commanded you, say, We are unprofitable servants: we have done that which was our duty to do.
LUKE 17:10 KJV

The concept of adhering to personal duty has fallen on hard times. Do what is right; do it on time and in the right spirit. Don't expect excessive praise or special notice. It's enough to know you have done what is right.

*Jesus said, "This sickness will not end in death.
No, it is for God's glory so that God's Son
may be glorified through it."*
JOHN 11:4

We have little idea what God may have in
mind when we go through troubling times or
face losses and sorrow. Our perspective is
necessarily limited, and we simply want it to
end. But God has purposes for everything,
and His glory is the ultimate result.

DAY
248

Jesus told her, "I am the resurrection and the life. Anyone who believes in me will live, even after dying. Everyone who lives in me and believes in me will never ever die. Do you believe this, Martha?"
JOHN 11:25–26 NLT

This is one of the high-water marks in the Gospels. What a ringing affirmation of Jesus' power and purpose for you! We will each die, but what we experience will be eternal life.

Jesus wept.
JOHN 11:35 KJV

No words are needed to convey the depth
of caring that calls for tears. Often silence
is more powerful communication than a
waterfall of words. Remember this as you
have opportunity to comfort the bereaved.

"Take away the stone."
JOHN 11:39

It would have been an easy thing for Jesus to command the stone to move, or to speak it into oblivion. But that is not the way He generally works. He asks you to live out your faith by doing what you can, and then He does the rest.

*"What sorrow awaits you Pharisees! For
you love to sit in the seats of honor in the
synagogues and receive respectful greetings as
you walk in the marketplaces. Yes, what sorrow
awaits you! For you are like hidden graves in a
field. People walk over them without knowing
the corruption they are stepping on."*
LUKE 11:43–44 NLT

The picture presented by Lazarus, alive and
walking, but still bound and constricted
by the signs of burial, is very helpful. Don't
allow yourself to be tied down by old
habits, bound by recurring sins, or crippled
by guilt. Jesus sets you free of all that!
Live in your freedom.

DAY
252

*And Jesus answering said, Were there not
ten cleansed? but where are the nine?*
LUKE 17:17 KJV

Gratitude has always been in short supply.
Model yourself today on the one who
returned to thank Jesus for His healing.
Seek to be an expert in saying, "Thank
you," both to God and the people
around you.

*"The kingdom of God does not come with your
careful observation, nor will people say,
'Here it is,' or 'There it is,' because the
kingdom of God is within you."*
LUKE 17:20–21

The arena of God's government and rule
is within you. Don't look for His perfect
rule in any nation, political party, church, or
community. Do seek to make the kingdom
of your heart a place where He is allowed
to reign as Lord and King.

DAY
254

"When the Son of Man returns, it will be like it was in Noah's day. In those days, the people enjoyed banquets and parties and weddings right up to the time Noah entered his boat and the flood came and destroyed them all."
LUKE 17:26–27 NLT

When people are caught up in daily routines and captured by the rhythms of life, it is easy to forget that someday there will be an accounting. Someday the Lord Jesus shall return and the scroll of time will be rolled up. Live for eternity.

I tell you, this man went down to his house justified rather than the other: for every one that exalteth himself shall be abased; and he that humbleth himself shall be exalted.
LUKE 18:14 KJV

Repetition is the teacher's method of reinforcing a lesson that is hard to learn. Humility is not instinctive. It is not intuitive. It must be learned and relearned. So Jesus repeats it again and again, and we learn humility again and again.

*At the beginning the Creator 'made them
male and female,' and said, 'For this reason
a man will leave his father and mother
and be united to his wife, and the two will
become one flesh.' So they are no longer
two, but one. Therefore what God has
joined together, let man not separate."*
MATTHEW 19:4–6

The hardest part for many marriages is
leaving the past behind. Allegiance to
mother and father are now trumped by love
for a spouse. Separation and divorce are,
sadly, more prevalent when one or both
partners cannot escape the shadows
of the past.

But Jesus said, "Let the children come to me. Don't stop them! For the Kingdom of Heaven belongs to those who are like these children."
MATTHEW 19:14 NLT

It is jokingly said that children and dogs are good judges of character. Children were drawn to Jesus. They sensed His love, understanding, and acceptance; and they yearned for the consistency of His character and the justice of His demands.

Then Jesus beholding him loved him, and
said unto him, One thing thou lackest:
go thy way, sell whatsoever thou hast,
and give to the poor, and thou shalt have
treasure in heaven: and come, take up
the cross, and follow me.
MARK 10:21 KJV

Jesus has an uncanny way of putting His
finger on a person's area of weakness.
In this instance it was a young man held
in thrall by his possessions. Whatever
holds you captive must be broken up and
dispersed so that you can follow Jesus
wholeheartedly.

*Jesus looked around and said to his disciples,
"How hard it is for the rich to enter
the kingdom of God!"*
MARK 10:23

I'm glad Jesus didn't say it is impossible!
Difficult, yes, but not impossible. Riches
cast the illusion of self-sufficiency and
lasting security, and make it more difficult
for a person to see the need for a Savior.
Don't permit yourself to be caught
in the spell of this illusion.

*Jesus looked at them intently and said,
"Humanly speaking, it is impossible. But not
with God. Everything is possible with God."*
MARK 10:27 NLT

God specializes in things considered
impossible. Is there anything in your life
that looms as an immovable object, an
impassable barrier? Begin today to talk
with God about it. Is there an impossible
person in your way or an unbreakable
habit you cannot shake? Trust Him and
wait patiently.

And Jesus answered and said, Verily I say unto you, There is no man that hath left house, or brethren, or sisters, or father, or mother, or wife, or children, or lands, for my sake, and the gospel's, but he shall receive an hundredfold now in this time, houses, and brethren, and sisters, and mothers, and children, and lands, with persecutions; and in the world to come eternal life.
MARK 10:29–30 KJV

For every demand Jesus puts upon you, there are enormous compensations in this life and beyond. The cost of following Jesus today may seem to you to be too high to bear. Don't quit; don't defect. Don't stop following Him. Payday is still to come!

DAY
262

*"But many who are first will be last,
and the last first."*
MARK 10:31

Long before the story of the tortoise and
the hare, Jesus knew that life assessment
is made at the end, not the beginning of
life. No matter how spiritually deprived
your beginning, you can now thrive in your
relationship with Jesus.

But Jesus called them together and said, "You know that the rulers in this world lord it over their people, and officials flaunt their authority over those under them. But among you it will be different. Whoever wants to be a leader among you must be your servant."
MATTHEW 20:25–26 NLT

Conventional wisdom is not always right. The ways of business and government do not apply to spiritual leadership. Find where people hurt and set out to help. In so doing, you will discover an authority not conveyed by title or by pomp and circumstance.

*Even as the Son of man came not to be
ministered unto, but to minister, and to give
his life a ransom for many.*
MATTHEW 20:28 KJV

The purpose of Jesus' life is not to be
found in the relatively few He healed. Nor is
it discovered in His teachings that continue
to help many. Rather, it is in the giving of
Himself to redeem all who believe, that we
find His life purpose.

"What do you want me to do for you?"
MARK 10:51

Quick answers to this question may not
be the best answers. It is no easy task to
uncover inner depths and identify our true
needs. Only rarely is our deepest need one
of pressing, immediate concern. What do
you want Jesus to do for you? Really?

*And Jesus said to him, "Go, for your faith
has healed you." Instantly the man could
see, and he followed Jesus down the road.*
MARK 10:52 NLT

It takes as much faith to go as it does to
come to Jesus. It is away from the noise
and heat of life that we most often meet
Jesus and find healing for our damaged
emotions and forgiveness for our sins.
But then He sends us back healed and
restored to face the clamor of life again.

And when Jesus came to the place, he looked up, and saw him, and said unto him, Zacchaeus, make haste, and come down; for to day I must abide at thy house.
LUKE 19:5 KJV

Are you hiding from Jesus? He knows where you are and desires your immediate response. He wishes to live in you all day long and bless your life with His presence and peace. Come out of hiding and go with Him today.

*"For the Son of Man came to seek and
to save what was lost."*
LUKE 19:10

Jesus had laserlike clarity about His
purpose and mission. Because He
succeeded in His, we have the privilege of
joining Him in seeking out those who are in
need. The world is full of people groping for
help and hope. Introduce them to Jesus.

But as he came closer to Jerusalem and saw the city ahead, he began to weep. "How I wish today that you of all people would understand the way to peace. But now it is too late, and peace is hidden from your eyes."
LUKE 19:41–42 NLT

Most cities would cause Jesus to weep today. Inside are multitudes of people trying to find peace. They repeatedly find themselves on dead-end streets, no closer than before to inner peace. And all the time the peace that Jesus gives is hidden, sometimes by sinful lives, more often by reluctant Christians.

*And said unto them, It is written, My house
shall be called the house of prayer; but ye
have made it a den of thieves.*
MATTHEW 21:13 KJV

It is very easy to turn to our personal
benefit what really belongs to God.
Perhaps the easiest way to "cleanse the
temple" is to restore prayer to its place
of importance. Find a church that values
prayer and practices it, and you will be
on the right track.

"The hour has come for the Son of Man to be glorified. I tell you the truth, unless a kernel of wheat falls to the ground and dies, it remains only a single seed. But if it dies, it produces many seeds."
JOHN 12:23–24

The miracle of multiplication lies in giving yourself to God and His work. As you do so, you will often be amazed—either in this life or assuredly in the life to come—of the far-reaching effects of living for Jesus.

"Anyone who wants to be my disciple must follow me, because my servants must be where I am. And the Father will honor anyone who serves me."
JOHN 12:26 NLT

The call to faithful living lies not so much in some future honor bestowed by the heavenly Father, but in the promise of Jesus that we shall be with Him. That is honor enough to motivate you to follow closely.

*Then Jesus said unto them, Yet a little while
is the light with you. Walk while ye have the
light, lest darkness come upon you: for he that
walketh in darkness knoweth not whither he
goeth. While ye have light, believe in the light,
that ye may be the children of light. These
things spake Jesus, and departed,
and did hide himself from them.*
JOHN 12:35–36 KJV

In spite of constant teaching, the disciples
seemingly had no comprehension of what
was coming. The betrayal and the cross
took them by surprise. Jesus' warning to
walk in the light while they could is a helpful
reminder to us to do what we can
while we still can.

DAY
274

*"For I did not speak of my own accord,
but the Father who sent me commanded
me what to say and how to say it. I know
that his command leads to eternal life.
So whatever I say is just what the Father
has told me to say."*
JOHN 12:49–50

This kind of close obedience should be
our daily goal. Do what He commands, go
where He leads, speak what He says, and
be what He enables. That is Christlike living
that pleases the Father greatly.

*"I tell you, you can pray for anything, and if you
believe that you've received it, it will be yours."*
MARK 11:24 NLT

Put aside, for all time, questions about
what this means. Consider instead, the
impossibility of receiving anything from
God while in an unbelieving, unexpecting,
disobedient mind-set. Believe and receive.

DAY 276

And when ye stand praying, forgive, if ye have ought against any: that your Father also which is in heaven may forgive you your trespasses.
MARK 11:25 KJV

God will often use our times of prayer to remind us of things left unfinished in our lives. This is especially true of unmerciful attitudes and ungracious thoughts. These reminders are merciful acts of God, allowing us to clear our consciences before Him.

"Bring me a denarius and let me look at it." They brought the coin, and he asked them, "Whose portrait is this? And whose inscription?" "Caesar's," they replied. Then Jesus said to them, "Give to Caesar what is Caesar's and to God what is God's."
MARK 12:15 –17

We are bound to pay our taxes, obey the laws of the land, and live as good citizens. But because we also bear the image of God in our own beings, we are to give ourselves to God. We are His by right of creation, His by redemption (for Jesus died for us), and His by donation, for we give ourselves to Him.

DAY
278

Jesus replied, "Your mistake is that you don't know the Scriptures, and you don't know the power of God."
MARK 12:24 NLT

It is very unlikely that you will know the power of God without knowing the scriptures. Make the scriptures your lifelong project and your daily quest. Read the Bible daily, read all the way through the Bible, until the scriptures take root in your soul.

*And Jesus answered him, The first of all the
commandments is, Hear, O Israel; The Lord our
God is one Lord: and thou shalt love the Lord
thy God with all thy heart, and with all thy soul,
and with all thy mind, and with all thy strength:
this is the first commandment.*
MARK 12:29–30 KJV

Hold nothing back from God. Hold nothing
in reserve. Make no effort to conserve
for later what you can give Him now. He
desires to have all there is of you so that
He may fill you with Himself, and reflect
Himself in you, to others.

DAY
280

"The second [commandment] is this: 'Love your neighbor as yourself.' There is no commandment greater than these."
MARK 12:31

Only as God fills you with Himself can you truly carry out this command with consistency and without grudging. Your neighbor is to be holy in your eyes, worthy of your best.

*Realizing how much the man understood,
Jesus said to him, "You are not far from the
Kingdom of God." And after that, no one dared
to ask him any more questions.*
MARK 12:34 NLT

To be close to the kingdom of God can
mean you are ready to accept God's rule
in your life. It can also mean you come
achingly close without ever experiencing
His benevolent rule. Which way are you
facing? Toward God? Or have you
turned your back on Him?

Then spake Jesus to the multitude, and to his disciples, saying, The scribes and the Pharisees sit in Moses' seat: all therefore whatsoever they bid you observe, that observe and do; but do not ye after their works: for they say, and do not.
MATTHEW 23:1–3 KJV

It is a terrible indictment to be told that our deportment fails to match our teaching. The worst kind of internal dissonance is created when life and lip are not connected. Seek God's enabling to live out all you commend so that your life is a harmony of peace.

*"You are not to be called 'Rabbi,' for you have
only one Master and you are all brothers. And
do not call anyone on earth 'father,' for you
have one Father, and he is in heaven."*
MATTHEW 23:8–9

Don't become anyone's devotee or disciple.
Follow Jesus only and obey Him. Learn from
others, respect and honor them, but do not
put them in the place of God, who will
not share His glory with others.

DAY
284

"What sorrow awaits you teachers of religious law and you Pharisees. Hypocrites! For you are careful to tithe even the tiniest income from your herb gardens, but you ignore the more important aspects of the law—justice, mercy, and faith. You should tithe, yes, but do not neglect the more important things."
MATTHEW 23:23 NLT

It is easy to focus on the externals of religion and think that we have fulfilled our duty. Even those duties that involve a measure of self-sacrifice, like giving a tithe of our income, are easier than dealing with the core issues of obedience and love.

Woe unto you, scribes and Pharisees, hypocrites! for ye make clean the outside of the cup and of the platter, but within they are full of extortion and excess.
MATTHEW 23:25 KJV

Many a person appears to be an upstanding member of the community. It's only when a crisis arises or there comes a call for public disclosure of personal information that the truth is revealed. Live so that if your most secret dealings were revealed, you could hold your head high.

DAY
286

*"On the outside you appear to people as
righteous but on the inside you are full of
hypocrisy and wickedness."*
MATTHEW 23:28

Reputation is what people think you are.
Character is what God knows you to be on
the inside. You cannot always control your
reputation, and only rarely should you focus
on improving or preserving it. Focus, rather,
on character; and reputation will follow
in its wake.

*While Jesus was in the Temple, he watched
the rich people dropping their gifts
in the collection box.*
LUKE 21:1 NLT

If we thought our gifts were being
monitored, we would protest and call it
"invasion of privacy." Jesus saw not only
the gift but the resources from which they
were drawn. He still sees! He knows the
motivation as well as the act.

And he saw also a certain poor widow casting in thither two mites. And he said, Of a truth I say unto you, that this poor widow hath cast in more than they all: for all these have of their abundance cast in unto the offerings of God: but she of her penury hath cast in all the living that she had.
LUKE 21:2–4 KJV

The best way to measure your giving is by how much is left over after the gift is given! Some would say to give until it hurts. Others say to give until it helps. In any case, give, knowing that the real accounting takes place in heaven.

*"At that time many will turn away from the
faith and will betray and hate each other,
and many false prophets will appear
and deceive many people."*
MATTHEW 24:10–11

Note the cascading negative effects of
turning away from the faith. Trust is the first
casualty, and where trust is gone, hatred
creeps in to destroy relationships. Spiritual
falsehood and deceit take the advantage,
and people are hurt.

DAY
290

"Sin will be rampant everywhere, and the love of many will grow cold. But the one who endures to the end will be saved."
MATTHEW 24:12–13 NLT

In spiritual issues, as in so much else, what counts most is persistence, tenacity, continuance. This is a long-distance marathon, not a dash that will be over in a moment. What matters most is not speed but endurance. Don't allow your love to cool.

And this gospel of the kingdom shall be preached in all the world for a witness unto all nations; and then shall the end come.
MATTHEW 24:14 KJV

When will come the wrap-up to history? When will Jesus return? Many fanciful and false answers have been given, but of this you can be certain: The gospel will be preached everywhere, to all nations. Your obedience to the Great Commission is part of the answer.

*"For false Christs and false prophets will
appear and perform signs and miracles to
deceive the elect—if that were possible.
So be on your guard; I have told you
everything ahead of time."*
MARK 13:22–23

Signs and miracles are not the ultimate
proof of an authentic ministry. Don't be
misled by showmanship and exaggerated
claims of success. Look for such things
as humility, joy, self-control, peace, and
faithfulness; and you will not be led astray.

DAY
293

"Heaven and earth will disappear, but my words will never disappear."
MATTHEW 24:35 NLT

The enduring quality of the Bible is well-documented. Tyrants and skeptics have tried to do away with it, sought to have it banned and discredited. But year after year it continues to sell in more languages and greater quantity than any other book. Don't be content just to have a Bible; read it!

And take heed to yourselves, lest at any time your hearts be overcharged with surfeiting, and drunkenness, and cares of this life, and so that day come upon you unawares.
LUKE 21:34 KJV

"The cares of life" is a catch-all phrase for everything that brings a shadow to block the presence of God in your life. Think about what cares weigh upon you today. Consider carefully how you can commit your way to the Lord so that attention can be returned to God and His deliverance.

"So you also must be ready, because the Son of Man will come at an hour when you do not expect him."
MATTHEW 24:44

Jesus is coming! It might even be today! Has this great hope grown dim in your life? Be ready and alert for His coming so that at any hour you are ready to welcome Jesus back to earth as Master and Lord.

DAY
296

"The master was full of praise. 'Well done, my good and faithful servant. You have been faithful in handling this small amount, so now I will give you many more responsibilities. Let's celebrate together!'"
MATTHEW 25:21 NLT

Faithfulness in small matters prepares us step-by-step for greater things. What you do today for Jesus' sake may seem small and insignificant, hardly worth doing at all. But do it well, do it faithfully, and know you share His happiness in you!

DAY
297

*When the Son of man shall come in his glory,
and all the holy angels with him, then shall he
sit upon the throne of his glory: and before
him shall be gathered all nations: and he shall
separate them one from another, as a shepherd
divideth his sheep from the goats: and he shall
set the sheep on his right hand,
but the goats on the left.*
MATTHEW 25:31–33 KJV

For as long as history has been recorded,
nations have been at each other's throats.
What a scene this will be, when all people
and nations pay homage to Jesus. It's
sobering to realize that such a day will
mean righteous judgment as well.

DAY
298

*"'I tell you the truth, whatever you did for
one of the least of these brothers of mine,
you did for me.'"*
MATTHEW 25:40

Investment in the lives of the weak and
powerless can be misunderstood and
misconstrued. But it will not go unrewarded
by the Lord, who identifies Himself most
closely with those who are shunned and
marginalized. No one is "least" in His eyes.

DAY
299

*"And they will go away into eternal punishment,
but the righteous will go into eternal life."*
MATTHEW 25:46 NLT

Perfect justice in this life is never realized.
Guilty people get off scot-free, and we cry out
against the unfairness. If there were no final
judgment in the world to come, this life could
seem futile. God has declared that He holds
the scales of judgment. The alternatives are
stark but ultimately comforting.

For ye have the poor always with you;
but me ye have not always.
MATTHEW 26:11 KJV

The earthly ministry of Jesus lasted
only about three years. His followers of
necessity attended to Him. We have now
had two thousand years to carry on His
work, and still there are people needing
help and crying out for hope. Let's be
about the right work today.

DAY
301

"I tell you the truth, wherever this gospel is preached throughout the world, what she has done will also be told, in memory of her."
Matthew 26:13

Simple acts, done for Jesus, have the potential to live on long after life is done. What you do today in Jesus' name may have consequences far larger than you can imagine. Don't try to manipulate the consequences; focus on the acts!

*Jesus told them, "In this world the kings
and great men lord it over their people, yet
they are called 'friends of the people.' But
among you it will be different. Those who
are the greatest among you should take
the lowest rank, and the leader should be
like a servant."*
LUKE 22:25–26 NLT

Think for a moment about the
consequences of a bad example. Who
wants to be held up as an illustration of
how *not* to live? Strive to live with humility
and trust, serving others.

Peter saith unto him, Thou shalt never wash my feet. Jesus answered him, If I wash thee not, thou hast no part with me.
JOHN 13:8 KJV

It's never wise to say no to Jesus! The stakes are much too high, and the alternative is grim. Say yes to Jesus today, and allow Him to cleanse and guide you. Make His will yours today and every day.

DAY
304

*"You call me 'Teacher' and 'Lord,'
and rightly so, for that is what I am.
Now that I, your Lord and Teacher,
have washed your feet, you also
should wash one another's feet."*
JOHN 13:13–14

Jesus does more than set a high
standard or make suggestions or issue
recommendations that can be accepted
or rejected. He is our Lord. And as such,
He is to be obeyed and followed.

*"I have given you an example to follow.
Do as I have done to you."*
JOHN 13:15 NLT

Jesus will never ask of you what He has
not Himself already done. If He calls you to
a place of humble service, it is because He
has served you. You will never go wrong
observing His example and following Him.

*A new commandment I give unto you, That
ye love one another; as I have loved you,
that ye also love one another.*
JOHN 13:34 KJV

Human love narrows down. Divine love
broadens out. Perhaps our natural loves
are so selective and exclusive that we need
His Word to open our eyes and broaden
our scope to include all God's family
in our love.

DAY
307

"By this all men will know that you are my disciples, if you love one another."
JOHN 13:35

The mark of true discipleship is deceptively simple and uncomplicated. Because real love is hard, we have made substitutes of doctrinal accuracy, behavioral conformity, and political correctness. The result is an imperfect love and a prideful spirit.

*"Don't let your hearts be troubled.
Trust in God, and trust also in me."*
JOHN 14:1 NLT

Apparently we have some measure of
control over our own emotional state. The
way to shrug off a troubled heart is to
concentrate on a positive trust in the God
who loves you and the continuing life of
Jesus within you.

*And if I go and prepare a place for you,
I will come again, and receive you unto myself;
that where I am, there ye may be also.*
JOHN 14:3 KJV

To simply be in the presence of some
people is sheer joy. To know that you
are known by Jesus enough that He is
preparing a special place for you and will
spend time with you—ah, that is heaven!

"I am the way and the truth and the life. No one comes to the Father except through me."
JOHN 14:6

Many people part ways with Jesus at the point of exclusivity, being offended by the very nature of His claim. Those who follow Him all the way discover how valid and compelling His claim truly is.

"If you love me, obey my commandments."
JOHN 14:15 NLT

Asserting love and loyalty to Jesus means
nothing unless backed up by obedience in
thought, word, and deed. Anyone can talk
love for Jesus, but only a true disciple
wills to obey Him.

DAY
312

And I will pray the Father, and he shall give
you another Comforter, that he may abide
with you for ever.
JOHN 14:16 KJV

As you follow Jesus, you are never alone.
In the toughest spot and in the loneliest
moment, the Spirit of Jesus is with you to
assure you of God's love and to guide you
into His truth. When all others fail you,
you can depend on God's Spirit.

DAY
313

"The Counselor, the Holy Spirit, whom the Father will send in my name, will teach you all things and will remind you of everything I have said to you."
JOHN 14:26

One thing true of all humans is the need for lifetime learning and constant review. Thus, the provision of God perfectly meets the predicament of humanity. Ask the Holy Spirit to be your teacher and post reminder notes on your heart today.

DAY 314

"I am leaving you with a gift—peace of mind and heart. And the peace I give is a gift the world cannot give."
JOHN 14:27 NLT

The best peace the world can give is incomplete, partial, and intermittent. If the peace you have experienced seems always to be broken by bouts of conflict and fits of anger, then seek today for the lasting peace Jesus gives. His peace in your heart makes for a peaceful home and family.

Let not your heart be troubled,
neither let it be afraid.
JOHN 14:27 KJV

The problem of a troubled, fearful heart
is not always caused by circumstances
beyond our control. Much of the time it is
caused by inner responses that need to be
brought under the control of the Holy Spirit.
To that degree you can live an
untroubled, fearless life.

DAY
316

"I am the true vine, and my Father is the gardener. He cuts off every branch in me that bears no fruit, while every branch that does bear fruit he prunes so that it will be even more fruitful."
JOHN 15:1–2

The things in your life that are pinching you may be God's way of pruning away what is dead or dying. The pain of cutting always precedes the healing that leads to more fruitful living. Jesus intends for every part of your life to bear fruit.

*"Remain in me, and I will remain in you.
For a branch cannot produce fruit if it is
severed from the vine, and you cannot be
fruitful unless you remain in me."*
JOHN 15:4 NLT

Occasionally a severed branch will bud,
showing false signs of life. It will never bear
fruit, however, because it is separated from
the essential life of the vine. "Oh God, let
me live this day in union with you, and so
be an instrument of your life in the world."

I am the vine, ye are the branches: He
that abideth in me, and I in him, the same
bringeth forth much fruit: for without me
ye can do nothing.
JOHN 15:5 KJV

Too many Christians live as though they
can do almost everything by themselves,
reserving God's help for the extreme
tests only. The reality is that to live a fully
successful, productive life, you need Him in
every way to fill each day.

"This is to my Father's glory, that you bear much fruit, showing yourselves to be my disciples."
JOHN 15:8

There are no "great Christians." There are only Christians who walk so faithfully with Jesus that they reflect the Father's glory. The greatness belongs to God, and any greatness is a reflection of His glory. Your part this day is to stay close to Jesus, the source of power.

"I have loved you even as the Father has loved me. Remain in my love."
JOHN 15:9 NLT

God's love for you in Jesus is constant and unswerving. If it seems otherwise, you can be sure that somewhere you have stepped out of obedience and fellowship with Him. Step back into His love and be secure in Him.

*These things have I spoken unto you,
that my joy might remain in you,
and that your joy might be full.*
JOHN 15:11 KJV

Don't fall prey to the lie that following Jesus
will make your life miserable or cheat you
of true happiness. His purpose for you is to
experience an inner joy not dependent on
circumstance or change. In your walk with
God, don't stop short of complete joy.

DAY
322

"Greater love has no one than this, that he lay down his life for his friends."
JOHN 15:13

The cross is always a reminder of how much God loves you, of how limitless His determination is to bless you, and of how great is the company of friends with whom He surrounds you.

*"You didn't choose me. I chose you.
I appointed you to go and produce lasting fruit,
so that the Father will give you whatever you
ask for, using my name."*
JOHN 15:16 NLT

On days when your resolve to follow
Jesus wavers or even seems to disappear,
you can take comfort in knowing that
before you ever chose to follow Jesus, He
chose you. You have been selected and
appointed to bear abundant fruit.

*Nevertheless I tell you the truth; It is
expedient for you that I go away: for if I go
not away, the Comforter will not come unto
you; but if I depart, I will send him unto you.*
JOHN 16:7 KJV

It must have seemed strange to the
disciples to hear that Jesus' departure
would work to their benefit. But the coming
of the Holy Spirit means that all believers
everywhere can always experience the
presence of God in their day-to-day lives.
You cannot run or hide where God is not.

"When he comes, he will convict the world of guilt in regard to sin and righteousness and judgment: in regard to sin, because men do not believe in me."
JOHN 16:8–9

We classify sins as mortal or venial, as mere misdemeanors in God's eyes, as felonies or capital crimes—thus making some worse than others. We forget that only the sin of failing to believe in Jesus brings true guilt. Have you believed?

"Righteousness is available because I go to the Father, and you will see me no more."
JOHN 16:10 NLT

The bottom line to this world has already been determined: God has the final word, and judgment is pronounced against the evil one. Satan is still active and may seem to prevail, but his sentence is sure, and his time is limited. Those who follow him end in hell.

I have yet many things to say unto you,
but ye cannot bear them now. Howbeit when
he, the Spirit of truth, is come, he will guide you
into all truth: for he shall not speak of himself;
but whatsoever he shall hear, that shall he
speak: and he will shew you things to come.
JOHN 16:12–13 KJV

You can expect a lifetime of learning as God
the Holy Spirit opens up truth as you are
able to bear it. His guidance is sure, and He
will not rest until you reach full maturity.

DAY
328

*"Until now you have not asked for anything
in my name. Ask and you will receive,
and your joy will be complete."*
JOHN 16:24

So many prayers are repetitive, rote, and
boring; it's no wonder so few are answered!
Jesus invites you to take prayer to a new
level, to invoke His name and nature and
enter into a mature joy.

*"For the Father himself loves you dearly
because you love me and believe that I came
from God. Yes, I came from the Father into the
world, and now I will leave the world
and return to the Father."*
JOHN 16:27–28 NLT

Believing in Jesus ushers you into a whole
network of love, not the least of which is
the love of God the Father. You can enter
into the most difficult aspect of your life
confident and secure in His love. When the
time comes to leave this world, you can
have confidence because He who
loves you has gone ahead.

DAY 330

These things I have spoken unto you, that in me ye might have peace. In the world ye shall have tribulation: but be of good cheer; I have overcome the world.
JOHN 16:33 KJV

You can be an island of peace in an ocean of trouble! But you can't do it by yourself. Christ Himself, living in you today, has overcome all the evil forces arrayed against you, and He will spread His peace throughout your life.

DAY
331

"Now this is eternal life: that they may know you, the only true God, and Jesus Christ, whom you have sent."
JOHN 17:3

Eternal life is a present possession and not just a future hope. In knowing God through faith in His Son, Jesus Christ, you have, right now, the life of the eternal!

DAY 332

"My prayer is not for the world, but for those you have given me, because they belong to you."
JOHN 17:9 NLT

It is awesome to realize that Jesus prays to the Father—for you! You are the special object of His prayers. You would feel blessed to have a famous Christian pray for you, doubly blessed to have an authentically holy person pray. So take courage today knowing that Christ has prayed for you.

DAY
333

And now I am no more in the world, but these are in the world, and I come to thee. Holy Father, keep through thine own name those whom thou hast given me, that they may be one, as we are.
JOHN 17:11 KJV

Once again, Jesus emphasized Christian unity. The focus of His prayers to the Father, the reason for divine protection, and the purpose for God's power are to bring to unity the whole family of God.

DAY 334

"My prayer is not that you take them out of the world but that you protect them from the evil one."
JOHN 17:15

God's will and plan are not to isolate you from evil but to insulate you from harm. You may be surrounded by evil people and attacked by evil thoughts, but you are safe in His protection. He is praying for you.

DAY
335

*"Make them holy by your truth;
teach them your word, which is truth."*
JOHN 17:17 NLT

In the battle for integrity and personal
holiness, the greatest weapon you have
is the Word of God. Read it daily. Seek to
understand it. Apply it to your life.
It will change you!

DAY 336

As thou hast sent me into the world, even so have I also sent them into the world.
JOHN 17:18 KJV

You will never go anywhere Jesus has not already been. Long before you were ever sent on a mission of service, Jesus came into the world to serve and to sacrifice Himself. Think about where He might want you to serve Him this day.

"My prayer is not for them alone. I pray also for those who will believe in me through their message, that all of them may be one, Father, just as you are in me and I am in you. May they also be in us so that the world may believe that you have sent me."
JOHN 17:20–21

The purpose of prayer goes far deeper than your personal happiness and convenience. God's heart is for the whole world — past, present, and still to be born. If in the process of leading others to believe in Jesus you have your needs and wants supplied, consider yourself blessed, but the goal is for the world to believe.

*He told them, "My soul is crushed with grief
to the point of death. Stay here and keep
watch with me."*
MATTHEW 26:38 NLT

When you feel most desperately alone
and in need of a thoughtful companion,
don't think it a weakness. It is rather a part
of your humanity, a part that Jesus, the
perfect human, experienced with the
same urgency you feel.

DAY
339

And he went a little further, and fell on his face, and prayed, saying, O my Father, if it be possible, let this cup pass from me: nevertheless not as I will, but as thou wilt.
MATTHEW 26:39 KJV

If today you face a task you dread, an exam you fear, a medical procedure you don't understand, then you have likely prayed this prayer of Jesus. In His mercy He sometimes provides an "out." More likely, though, He will give the grace and courage to drink the cup to the dregs.

DAY
340

"Keep watch and pray, so that you will not give in to temptation. For the spirit is willing, but the body is weak!"
MATTHEW 26:41 NLT

Only rarely does temptation do its deadly deed with suddenness and surprise. It insinuates, it flatters, it charms. It starts small and innocently. If you wait until it is fully grown, you wait too long! Watch and pray and turn your back early on, while both spirit and body can still say no.

*Then said Jesus unto him, Put up again thy
sword into his place: for all they that take the
sword shall perish with the sword.*
MATTHEW 26:52 KJV

About the best that violence can do is to
exchange one set of problems for another.
Religious people who fancy themselves to
be "defenders of the faith" or "crusaders for
justice" need especially to remember this.
Dial back the invective and turn up the love
for a better response.

DAY
342

*"Do you think I cannot call on my Father,
and he will at once put at my disposal more
than twelve legions of angels?"*
MATTHEW 26:53

We believers in Jesus have more hidden
resources than we dare believe! Go forward
today knowing this and believing that if and
when necessary, God can and will call out
His reserve forces to come to your aid. Live
today so as to make the devil fear!

DAY
343

But Jesus remained silent. Then the high priest said to him, "I demand in the name of the living God—tell us if you are the Messiah, the Son of God."
MATTHEW 26:63 NLT

It is more effective to say nothing, than to speak too soon, say too much, or talk without thinking. A person of few words is rarely tripped up by his speech. "God, help me today to know when to speak up and when to be silent. Amen."

Then said Jesus, Father, forgive them; for they know not what they do. And they parted his raiment, and cast lots.
LUKE 23:34 KJV

Ignorance is a poor defense for wrongdoing that rarely holds up in court. Most of the time we do know what we are doing, and as a consequence, we know we need forgiveness. The good news is that God will forgive because of what Jesus has done.

*About the ninth hour Jesus cried out in a loud
voice, "Eloi, Eloi, lama sabachthani?"
—which means, "My God, my God,
why have you forsaken me?"*
MATTHEW 27:46

Because Jesus went through the
staggering abyss of abandonment and
aloneness, you need never feel the futility of
loneliness. He has borne the whole weight
of the world's sin and now invites you to
eternal fellowship with Him.

DAY
346

*Then Pilate went back into his headquarters
and called for Jesus to be brought to him.
"Are you the king of the Jews?" he asked
him. Jesus replied, "Is this your own
question, or did others tell you about me?"*
JOHN 18:33–34 NLT

Ideas penetrate where armies never can.
Any show of force by the disciples would
have been crushed immediately and
without mercy. But someone told what he
or she knew of Jesus, and it quickly went
to the center of power. You can do the
same today.

DAY
347

And Jesus said unto him, Verily I say unto thee,
Today shalt thou be with me in paradise.
LUKE 23:43 KJV

The repentant thief had no time to clean
up his act or cover his tracks. He had
been caught, tried, sentenced, and hung.
He couldn't reform his ways or repay his
victims. He did the only thing he could. He
believed in Jesus and entered into life.

*When Jesus saw his mother there, and the
disciple whom he loved standing nearby,
he said to his mother, "Dear woman, here is
your son," and to the disciple, "Here is your
mother."*
JOHN 19:26–27

Whether dealing with a bereaved mother or
a lonely disciple, Jesus puts His followers
into community. No one makes it alone
in the family of God; we make it together.
Have you found your spiritual home and
family, and are you making that a priority?

DAY
349

Then Jesus shouted, "Father, I entrust my spirit into your hands!" And with those words he breathed his last.
LUKE 23:46 NLT

There is no better place to be than in the Father's hands. You can safely commit your hopes, dreams and, yes, your nightmares, to Him. Release your control and let God take over.

*When Jesus therefore had received the
vinegar, he said, It is finished: and he
bowed his head, and gave up the ghost.*
JOHN 19:30 KJV

Not till Jesus had finished His work of
redemption did He flinch or flag in His spirit.
But once finished, He willingly relinquished
His work. "God, make me to persevere till
my work on earth is ended, and then spare
me the frantic pace of one unwilling
to let go. Amen."

He said to them, "How foolish you are, and how slow of heart to believe all that the prophets have spoken! Did not the Christ have to suffer these things and then enter his glory?"
LUKE 24:25–26

Better to be "slow of heart" than to be hard-hearted. But better still to be ready at all times to listen, learn, and believe! Away with sluggishness of spirit! Now is the time to be engaged and understanding. Ask God to help you read and understand His Word, the Bible.

DAY
352

*And just as they were telling about it,
Jesus himself was suddenly standing there
among them. "Peace be with you," he said.*
LUKE 24:36 NLT

Fear, uncertainty, and weak faith often lead
to another study, a new seminar, and more
talk. What we need is for the risen Christ to
stand among us and pronounce His peace.
"Oh living Christ, let me this day know Your
peace and presence. Amen."

*And he said unto them, Why are ye troubled?
and why do thoughts arise in your hearts?
Behold my hands and my feet, that it is I
myself: handle me, and see; for a spirit hath
not flesh and bones, as ye see me have.*
LUKE 24:38–39 KJV

The resurrection changes everything!
Troubles become manageable and doubts
are settled when we are convinced that the
Jesus who lived and died is now alive. Take
the risen Christ into your day today.

DAY
354

Again Jesus said, "Peace be with you! As the Father has sent me, I am sending you."
JOHN 20:21

With great patience, Jesus repeatedly pronounced peace upon His disciples. He understands, then, how often we lack inner peace and how much we need His renewed blessing. If we are to go forth as His "sent ones," we ourselves must be at peace.

*Then he said to Thomas, "Put your finger here,
and look at my hands. Put your hand into the
wound in my side. Don't be faithless
any longer. Believe!"*
JOHN 20:27 NLT

Never be ashamed of your questions or
fearful of your doubts. Jesus entertains
honest doubt and treats your questions
with dignity. Work through your doubts until
you come again to a place of believing.

DAY
356

*Jesus saith unto him, Thomas, because
thou hast seen me, thou hast believed:
blessed are they that have not seen, and
yet have believed.*
JOHN 20:29 KJV

Only a tiny minority of the millions who
have believed through the centuries had
the privilege of seeing and hearing Jesus.
Should we (who have not) sometimes feel
shortchanged? Of course not! We, too,
sense His living presence in our lives.

*When they had finished eating, Jesus said to
Simon Peter, "Simon son of John, do you
truly love me more than these?"*
JOHN 21:15

Jesus has the right to challenge us on any
evidence of misplaced affection. Peter
loved to fish. Others love to golf. The issue
is, which love has the preeminent place
in your heart? "Lord, help me to
love You supremely. Amen."

DAY
358

*"Feed my lambs. . . . Take care of my
sheep. . . . Feed my sheep."*
JOHN 21:15–17 NLT

If you aspire to be a Christian leader,
remember that your role is to care for the
lambs. Humility, gentleness, patience,
and compassion are to be the controlling
qualities. Too often these are forgotten in
the rush to issue orders and form up the
troops. Don't bully the sheep. "Feed" them.

*And Jesus came and spake unto them, saying,
All power is given unto me in heaven and in
earth. Go ye therefore, and teach all nations,
baptizing them in the name of the Father, and
of the Son, and of the Holy Ghost.*
MATTHEW 28:18–19 KJV

Two thousand years have passed since this
clear, unambiguous command was given
to His followers. We can rap our knuckles
over our failure, or we can wrack our brains
to know how we can be involved in its
fulfillment. It's time to get the job done.

*"Teaching them to obey everything I have
commanded you. And surely I am with you
always, to the very end of the age."*
MATTHEW 28:20

As you have worked through this year with
Jesus, you have a better idea than most of
all that Jesus commanded His followers.
Because He is still with us, we can pass
His words along to a new generation
of Jesus followers.

*And he said, "Yes, it was written long ago that
the Messiah would suffer and die and rise from
the dead on the third day. It was also written
that this message would be proclaimed in
the authority of his name to all the nations,
beginning in Jerusalem: 'There is
forgiveness of sins for all who repent.'"*
LUKE 24:46–47 NLT

What begins at home (Jerusalem) is never
intended to stay there. The story of Jesus is
needed in every nation. The surest way to
stunt your continued growth as a Christian
is to focus all your energy on your "home."
There is still a world waiting!

DAY
362

And ye are witnesses of these things.
LUKE 24:48 KJV

God never intends us to report on what
we don't know or what we haven't
experienced. Share what He *has* done in
your life, and you will find Him doing even
more, which gives you still more to share.

DAY 363

"I am going to send you what my Father has promised; but stay in the city until you have been clothed with power from on high."
LUKE 24:49

Christians have never been intended to make progress on their own power. When they try, they fail. It's as simple as that. Only with power from on high—with God's might—can we find the needed strength.

DAY 364

He replied, "The Father alone has the authority to set those dates and times, and they are not for you to know. But you will receive power when the Holy Spirit comes upon you. And you will be my witnesses, telling people about me everywhere—in Jerusalem, throughout Judea, in Samaria, and to the ends of the earth."
ACTS 1:7–8 NLT

Precisely because we do not know times and dates for Christ's return, we are to busy ourselves about what we *do* know. The ends of the earth need to hear of Jesus. Get involved in missions!

I have shewed you all things, how that so labouring ye ought to support the weak, and to remember the words of the Lord Jesus, how he said, It is more blessed to give than to receive.
ACTS 20:35 KJV

To listen to our prayers and observe our hands, one would think that it's more blessed to receive! Give all you can whenever you can in every way you can, and you will discover the true blessedness Jesus spoke of.

SCRIPTURE INDEX

6:28–30—Day 82
6:31–32—Day 83
6:33—Day 84
6:34—Day 85
7:6—Day 91
7:7—Day 92
7:12—Day 93
7:13—Day 94
7:14—Day 95
7:15–16—Day 96
7:17–18—Day 97
7:19–20—Day 98
7:21—Day 99
8:13—Day 105
9:2—Day 22
9:9—Day 24
9:12—Day 25
9:28–29—Day 147
9:37—Day 149
9:38—Day 150
10:8—Day 151
10:16—Day 152
10:19–20—Day 153
10:22—Day 154
10:24–25—Day 155
10:28—Day 156
10:29–31—Day 157
10:38–39—Day 158
10:42—Day 159
11:20–21—Day 111
11:25—Day 112
11:27—Day 113
11:28—Day 114
11:29–30—Day 115
12:30—Day 120

12:31—Day 121
12:36—Day 122
12:39—Day 123
12:41—Day 124
13:9—Day 126
13:17—Day 127
13:27–28—Day 133
13:28–29—Day 134
13:44—Day 136
13:45—Day 137
13:47–49—Day 138
13:49–50—Day 139
14:26–27—Day 163
16:2–3—Day 173
16:4—Day 174
16:18—Day 176
17:20—Day 180
17:25–27—Day 181
18:2–4—Day 183
18:6—Day 184
18:15—Day 186
18:18—Day 187
18:19—Day 188
18:20—Day 189
18:21–22—Day 190
19:4–6—Day 256
19:14—Day 257
20:25–26—Day 263
20:28—Day 264
21:13—Day 270
23:1–3—Day 282
23:8–9—Day 283
23:23—Day 284
23:25—Day 285
23:28—Day 286

TOPICAL INDEX